Debrett's

GREAT BRITISH FAMILIES

Debrett's
GREAT BRITISH FAMILIES

HUGH MONTGOMERY~MASSINGBERD

Salem House Publishers
Topsfield, Massachusetts

Frontispiece:
Louisa Duchess of Abercorn photographed with over
100 of her descendants in July 1894

First published in United States
by Salem House Publishers, 1988, 462 Boston Street,
Topsfield, MA 01983

First published in Great Britain in 1988
by Webb & Bower (Publishers) Limited, Exeter, Devon
in association with Michael Joseph Limited
27 Wright's Lane, London W8 5TZ

Designed by Vic Giolitto

Production by Nick Facer/Rob Kendrew

Picture research by Anne-Marie Ehrlich

Text Copyright © 1988 Hugh Montgomery-Massingberd

Debrett Trade Mark Copyright
© 1988 Debrett's Peerage Limited

Library of Congress Cataloging-in-Publication Data

Montgomery-Massingberd, Hugh.
  Debrett's great British families.
    1. Great Britain—Nobility—History.
  2. Great Britain—Gentry—History. I. Title.
  II. Title: Great British families.
  HT653.G7M663 1988   305.5′22′0941   87–35631
  ISBN 0–88162–359–8

Typeset in Great Britain
by AB Typesetting, Exeter, Devon

Printed and bound in Great Britain
by Purnell Book Production Ltd, Paulton, Bristol

CONTENTS

CHAPTER I

BED-ROCK

BED-ROCK — as you will have observed, the title of this introductory chapter — has a number of useful meanings. First, there is the territorial connotation which is highly appropriate as land is surely the bed-rock of the great British families. Bed-rock also conveys the figurative sense of first principles, basic facts which should be straightened out before we embark on this grand tour of dynastic survivors.

While on the subject of definitions, what do we understand by the word 'great', as applied to British families? Important, superior, prominent — yes, yes, but this doesn't get us very far. Of high rank or position, noble — now we are getting somewhere. Titled, in other words?

No, not necessarily. To talk of just the dukes, marquesses, earls, viscounts barons — and even bunging in the baronets for good measure — is to refer only to the 'nobility', whereas the British sort of aristocracy has always extended beyond mere coronets to include untitled families. This untitled aristocracy is somehow very typical of Britain. The 'great commoner' is a peculiarly British phenomenon. How much grander, for instance, to be the 28th Mr Gentle to live on Gentle land than to be, say, the 2nd Lord Neasden, the son of a party political hack who was kicked upstairs to give someone else a seat. And yet, to take a narrow view, Mr Gentle is a commoner — indeed might even be called 'middle class' by a sociologist — whereas Lord Neasden is a nobleman.

Moreover, cutting right across the system of titles emanating from the British Crown are the Celtic chieftainships of Scotland and Ireland. To a Highland Scot, to be chief of one's clan is without question infinitely more important than to be a mere peer or a baronet. Cameron of Lochiel, for example, occupies a proud place in Scottish society, though he holds no hereditary title; he also happens to own 130,000 acres, incidentally, which is more than anyone apart from a handful of peers. The old clan system persisted in the Highlands for a while after the feudal system of land tenure had been introduced from the Continent into the Lowlands; and the old chieftainships and clan loyalties have survived down to the present day. As well as the chieftainships in Scotland there are also what are known as 'feudal baronies'. Although originating from the Crown, these are not actually peerages, but simply entitle their holders to be styled 'of' a particular place which they may either still own, or which they or their ancestors owned in the past.

The great families of Ireland also include a limited number of Chiefs of the name, recognized by the armorial authority in Dublin. These are the senior male descendants of potentates who were the independent rulers of various parts of Ireland when in the words of the old ballad 'the harp that once through Tara's Halls / The soul of music shed'.

By 'great' do we just mean 'rich', then? Certainly the only significant division that has existed in Britain between the greater and lesser aristocracy is not related to titles but to wealth. Families rich enough to be of national importance tend to form one group, families of only local importance, the other — the first group being, of course, very much smaller than the second. The first group has naturally always included most of the more illustrious families in the peerage, but it also includes wealthy baronets and rich untitled 'great commoners'.

In the second group, along with the untitled majority, can be placed most of the baronets, as well as a large number of peers of moderate means and rustic tastes. But the division between the wealthier and the less wealthy groups in the British aristocracy can be exaggerated, since the two groups have overlapped and intermarried. It should also be borne in mind that there have always been some comparatively poor families, historic, fashionable or influential enough to be counted in the first group, as well as families of great wealth which have never graduated beyond the second.

Various factors have served to emphasize the difference between the greater and lesser families of the aristocracy. The former were predominantly Whig, the latter Tory. The first group usually had, in addition to their country seats, fine town houses in London where they entertained lavishly during the season. The country landowners, in the second group, often possessed no metropolitan property at all. The younger sons from the lesser families had to earn their livings, while a higher proportion of the greater families' cadets tended to be — despite primogeniture — of independent means.

It is an interesting paradox, though, that the first group, for all its grandeur, was more closely connected with 'trade' than the second. The first group included in its number great banking and mercantile families like the Barings and Rothschilds and Hoares who never ceased to attend their offices in the City. Nineteenth-century dukes and marquesses were certainly not averse to going into partnerships with businessmen of plebeian origin in order to exploit the coal or ironstone on their estates. The 3rd Marquis of Bute, for instance, developed a harbour which he happened to own at Cardiff into a flourishing industrial port. And in the later nineteenth century, if a member of a great British family found himself less well off than he ought by rights to have been, he saved the situation by marrying into 'trade' in the form of an American heiress.

On the other hand, the second group would make careers in the services and professions rather than in business. Some proud and impoverished figures from these lesser families doubtless subscribed to the proverbial horror of 'trade'; but one suspects that this distaste for commerce was largely fostered by businessmen who had swiftly metamorphosed into squires, drawing the line immediately underneath them. The trade taboo is, in short, largely an historical myth.

But there is more to all this than money, or there should be. It can be argued that there is—or, at least, was—only one essential prerequisite for being counted among the British aristocracy: the right to be called a gentleman. This concept renders the distinction between nobility and gentry as meaningless. Even when Victorian society was at its most rigid, a duke and, say, an Indian army subaltern, both being gentlemen, were equal in class, however different they may have been in rank and wealth.

The difficulty lies, again, in expressing the meaning of 'gentleman'. Because of the complexity of the subject, the best definitions are of necessity cumbersome. They have to be something such as 'a man who occupies a certain place in society through birth, education, merit, wealth or rank, and also on account of his values, his manners, his courtesy, his magnanimity and his sense of honour'. This sort of definition becomes wide enough to accommodate a good or *gentle* man: gentle is certainly a useful word as it covers, in one sense, someone well born, well bred and entitled to bear arms, as well as having such attractive synonyms as kind, tender-hearted and amiable.

A coat of arms may be a badge of aristocracy; but it has never been necessary to have armorial bearings in order to be an aristocrat. Peerages, knighthoods, grants of arms and so forth have never done any more than give official confirmation of the recipient's status as a gentleman. Henry Peacham made this clear in his early seventeenth-century treatise on *The Compleat Gentleman*:

> Nobility being inherent and Naturall, can have (as the Diamond) the lustre not only from itselfe: honors and titles externally conferred are but attendant upon desert, and are but as apparell, and the Drapery to a beautiful body.

The Heralds, down to the present day, have recognized this fact by defining a gentleman as a man entitled to bear arms—in other words, a grant of arms is given to a man on the assumption that he is a gentleman already.

After the Heralds' Visitations of the late sixteenth and seventeenth centuries, when many of the long-established county families registered their

The title page of the second (1634) impression of Henry
Peacham's study of *The Compleat Gentleman* (first published
in 1622), a book which profoundly influenced his own and
subsequent generations. The author believed that a man
could be a gentleman through merit, regardless of birth—
giving as an example one Colonel Edmonds, 'a valiant
gentleman' who was the son of 'a poor baker of Edinburgh'.

pedigrees and coats of arms (which originated in the distinguishing marks of men in battle), there was something of a decline in grants of armorial bearings. The eighteenth century was not an age sympathetic to genealogy; Lord Chesterfield, for instance, commissioned, in a sarcastic gesture, portraits of 'Adam and Eve de Stanhope'. There was a trough of only 160 English grants made between 1730 and 1760, though there were a further 1,600 grants up to the end of the century. Well over 8,000 grants were recorded in the nineteenth century, however, and since then there have been notable increases in the 1920s, late 1940s and 1960s. Even today, the Kings of Arms, in that agreeable Queen Anne building, the College of Arms in the City of London, like to satisfy themselves that the 150 or so people to whom arms are granted each year are gentlemen. How they do so is another question.

The golden thread between the original meaning of 'gentle' as denoting good birth, and 'gentle' in its modern sense, as the opposite of rough and violent, is the medieval concept of chivalry. For if, by the end of the Middle Ages, wealth and position were beginning to count for more than ancestry in determining who was — and who was not — a gentleman, the idea was also gaining currency that to be a gentleman entailed certain obligations and the adherence to a certain code of behaviour. Although study of medieval chivalry shows that it never had a 'golden age' and that, despite the religious fervour of the Crusades, the perfect knight hardly existed outside romantic fiction, medieval chivalry can certainly be credited with having acted as a civilizing influence. More important than its immediate effect in the Middle Ages was its legacy to subsequent generations. The age of chivalry did not really bite the dust — or rather, the mud and filth, of the trenches — until 1914.

Back to bed-rock ('loose surface soil'): land. When sorting out the sheep from the goats — dividing up the greater and lesser families — landholdings are of paramount importance. As a rough generalization, it could be said in late-Victorian times that a landowner would have had to own upwards of 10,000 acres — and certainly more than 5,000 — to be in the wealthier group. Estates of over 100,000 acres were not unknown — the Duke of Devonshire, for instance, owned 140,000 acres in England and a further 60,000 acres in Ireland — and there were about a hundred English territorial magnates each owning more than 20,000 acres. At the opposite end of the scale, the smaller country squires who were the typical landowners in the less wealthy group would have owned estates of under 5,000 acres — in many cases not much more than the 1,000 acres which used sometimes to be thought of as the minimum required to qualify as 'landed gentry', though no such arbitrary rule ever existed.

Acreage, however, is not always a reliable guide to a landowner's standing and wealth. For example, the 1st Duke of Westminster's estates, a century ago, amounted to little more than 18,000 acres which would have put him

Colonel Sir Donald Cameron of Lochiel, 26th Chief of Clan
Cameron, one of the great territorial magnates of Britain,
at his family seat of Achnacarry, Inverness-shire. Lochiel
is almost unique among present-day representatives of great British families
in owning more land than was held by a predecessor
a century ago.

quite low among the territorial magnates. But he was, of course, one of the very richest peers of his time, owing to his London property. In Scotland and Ireland, estates tended to be larger than in England; though, since they frequently included vast tracts of mountain and other unproductive land, their revenues were generally small in relation to their size.

In 1883 Bateman published his much misused survey of *Great Landowners* which stated that thirty-odd peers possessed estates of over 100,000 acres. But only three — the Dukes of Devonshire, Northumberland and Cleveland — actually owned 100,000 or more English acres. The spectacular totals of the others were accounted for by acres and acres in Scotland and Ireland. Most of the 1,358,000 acres of the Duke of Sutherland, the largest Victorian landowner of all, was situated in the poor and remote Scottish county from which he took his title. His great wealth came not from these barren tracts but from the coal on his relatively modest 12,000 acres in Staffordshire.

A hundred years on, only fifteen per cent of the 'family estates' have survived in the same ownership. By county, the averages for survival range from six per cent for industrial or suburban counties, such as Surrey, to twenty-five per cent for a few of the rural areas like Devon and Shropshire. In Norfolk, for instance, although some 120 'family estates' remain, there have been forty demolitions of country houses this century and the break-up of some 110 estates.

But what is a 'family estate'? It can be defined broadly as an estate of upwards of 1,000 acres, with the following advantages: a country seat; an owner who has inherited from one or more earlier generations of his family; a family tradition of local responsibility and public office. In England today, on a rough calculation, there are at present about 1,600 such estates surviving (with 1,200 families having owned the estate for a least a century); as well as 150 in Wales; and 500 in Scotland.

This total of some 2,200 should be considered in relation to the number of family seats still in private occupation a century ago, namely 10,000 or so. It would seem that over three-quarters of these 2,200 'family estates' are under 5,000 acres in extent and about half come within the 1,000 to 2,000 bracket. Thus, those with anything like a claim to be considered 'territorial magnates' in these modern times cannot number more than a few hundred.

The merchant prince who sold up his business and established himself as a squire was following the traditional British rural rainbow. Critics of the aristocracy would maintain that many of its industrial recruits have not served the national interest by turning their backs on business. No doubt the passionate absorption in sporting activities on their estates perhaps went a little too far. But it can be argued that this love of the country is one of the strengths of the British aristocratic character. The country house — surely our greatest artistic achievement — is always regarded as 'home' by a great British family, even if there is also a town house. The aristocracies of some Conti-

Millais's portrait of the 8th Duke of Devonshire, the great
late-Victorian landowner who took part in politics simply
because he felt it to be his duty. His abilities tended
to be hidden by an air of somnolence — he is said to have
admitted to falling asleep in the middle of one of his
own speeches.

nental countries, on the other hand, tend to prefer their urban residences to their rural estates.

The great British families form a far less exclusive group than those in other European countries. To belong to the aristocracy in Britain it has never been necessary to possess the qualifications of sixteen heraldic quarterings or whatever; certificates of nobility have not yet been handed out to settle the matter. This very lack of rules has perhaps helped Britain to achieve the social fluidity which has been the vital ingredient in enabling the aristocracy to survive when so many of its European counterparts have become stratified and hamstrung by their outmoded caste-systems. The British sort of aristocracy has managed to avoid becoming a closed corporation and has always recruited itself from the outside. New blood has been gradually taken in — often so gradually as to be almost imperceptible — and this has prevented the sudden clamour for a blood transfusion. The great British families have always remained closely in touch with contemporary power and wealth.

In the Middle Ages, the aristocracy was in a strong enough position to be a rival to the Crown, but in Tudor and Stuart times it depended very much on royal favour. The great British families came nearest to being a closed corporation in the eighteenth century when the aristocracy was at its richest, most independent and most powerful. In the nineteenth century, however, the aristocracy was on a broader basis than at any other time. Now, through no choice of its own, the ranks have been closed again.

The basic historical difference between the sizes of the British aristocracy and the others is as follows: the British sort consisted of comparatively few titled families and a large number of untitled families; abroad, a much higher proportion of aristocratic families were titled. In Britain, it could be said that it was easy to join the aristocracy but difficult to get a title; abroad, titles were much more freely given.

And now some more basic facts, or simply statistics. Whereas, for instance, seventeenth-century Naples had some 119 princes, 156 dukes, 173 marquesses and almost countless counts, England at the end of that century could only claim 19 dukes, 3 marquesses and a total of 152 earls, viscounts and barons. There were, of course, no princes outside the royal family — as indeed there never have been. This factor has tended to increase the importance of the great families in Britain.

By 1900, the numbers of the British peerage — that is to say including peers of England, of Scotland, of Ireland, of Great Britain and of the United Kingdom — had risen to 673. From 1911 (the year in which the House of Lords was last threatened with the prospect of a flood of new creations similar to the current proposals of the erstwhile Viscount Stansgate) to 1983 (the year which saw the most new hereditary peerages) 628 more hereditary peerages were created. This remarkable increase during the present century has, however, been mostly confined to the two lowest ranks, of viscount and baron. Today there are some 900 hereditary peers and 1,200 baronets. We are not concerned with the life peers.

The ranks of the baronetage — the sixth rank in the hereditary system, so to speak — were swollen by the creation of 740 baronetcies at a fairly even rate between 1911 and 1965. Incidentally, why baronetcies have stopped being created is a mystery, as they do not, unlike peerages, confer any legislative powers. Is it simply a question of the hereditary principle now being regarded as unacceptable? In which case, what about the monarchy? It is especially sad to see the running down of a title associated with the traditional 'Bold Bad Bart' — a character not wholly to be trusted on the Turf or where a lady's virtue is concerned. One feels particularly sorry for the Lord Mayors of London who always used to rate a baronetcy. The honouring of leading City families in this way helped to emphasize the point that such professional dynasties, though they might have been landless, were just as much part of the hereditary aristocracy as the owners of ancestral acres.

Turning to the untitled county families, statistics are obviously not so cut and dried. These families have, however, been covered by *Burke's Landed Gentry* (eighteen editions, 1833–1972) and *Walford's County Families* (various editons, 1860–1920). The last three editions of the former featured some 3,800 landed (or formerly landed) untitled families, and a scholarly survey published by Michael Sayer in the *Genealogists' Magazine* reckoned that, as a series, *Burke's Landed Gentry* was about ninety per cent complete.

All these figures indicate the size of the field from which any choice of families has to be made. Inevitably any selection has to be pretty arbitrary.

It comes down to that word 'great' again. The trouble is, we all know what we think a 'great British family' is, rather in the same way we think we know what a 'gentleman' is, but what we think often cannot be put into words. And even if it could, it would not tally with everyone else's view on the subject.

There is, however, one vital synonym for 'great' and that is 'excellent'. Excellence concerns merit and can embrace dynasties from the 'intellectual aristocracy', such as the Wedgwood/Darwin network, who have never been territorial magnates, to the obvious heavy swells, such as the Cecils and the Churchills, who have turned out a series of national figures from their palatial estates.

The secret of the great British families is their knack of survival. They deserve attention as a social and economic phenomenon and as the creators of a magnificent heritage of country houses. What ultimately matters, though, is that they have continued for generation after generation to produce men and women of achievement. This is what really constitutes greatness.

CHAPTER II

OVER-MIGHTY SUBJECTS

THE END OF THE MIDDLE AGES

Jockey of Norfolk, be not too bold
For Dickon thy master is bought and sold.

As EVERY SCHOOLBOY should know from Shakespeare's *Richard III*, Sir John Howard, 1st Duke of Norfolk, did not take heed of this prophetic couplet which he found pinned to his tent the night before the Battle of Bosworth on that fateful day in August 1485. He was killed while leading the army of his royal master to whom he had been such a powerful servant. For all their vicissitudes, however, the 'ducal and illustrious' House of Howard has survived; but Bosworth Field, in the heart of England, saw the end of a remarkable number of great families.

The political and dynastic crises which erupted after 1455 into the civil wars known as the Wars of the Roses proved apocalyptic for the medieval aristocracy. The extinction and forfeiture of many of the more powerful families during these wars meant the disappearance of that medieval bogey, the 'over-mighty subject'. The victorious Henry VII brought in statutes against 'livery and maintenance', which made private armies illegal and, as the Middle Ages ended, the aristocracy no longer constituted any appreciable threat to the monarchy. The great feudal lord who was a rival to the Crown became virtually a back number after Bosworth.

It had, in fact, often been their royal blood as much as their private armies that had made the 'over-mighty subjects' so troublesome; Edward III's numerous sons had a lot to answer for in their descendants. But by the accession of the Tudors, the number of royal cadets and great lords of royal blood had much diminished through death, natural or violent. Henry VII and Henry VIII reduced the number still more by executing the last surviving Plantagenets. And in order to ensure that no members of the aristocracy would in future become too powerful through royal connections, the royal family, from the time of Henry VII onwards, tended to marry other royalties rather than British aristocrats. This custom prevailed until the present century when we have seen the future George VI marry Lady Elizabeth Bowes-Lyon, (now the Queen Mother), daughter of the Earl of Strathmore; his brother Prince Henry, Duke of Gloucester, marry Lady Alice Montagu-Douglas-Scott, daughter of the Duke of Buccleuch; and, of course, the present Prince of Wales bring back some more Stuart royal blood into the royal family by marrying Lady Diana Spencer.

Somehow, one cannot imagine Earl Spencer casting himself in the role of medieval bogeyman whatever unkind cracks may be levelled against the Princess of Wales's energetic stepmother. The last instance of an usurpation in the medieval tradition was the ill-fated intervention of Lady Jane Grey, whose mother's royal blood was of greater significance in this unhappy episode than the fact that her father was behaving like a throwback to the 'over-mighty subject'. In the event, the game was up for that somewhat priggish nine-days' queen as soon as the rightful sovereign, Mary Tudor, arrived in London.

It can be argued that the story of the great 'British' families effectively starts in the Tudor age, for the aristocracy as we know it today — or in the recent past — only began to take shape then. Basically the 'British' aristocracy is the English aristocratic system extended over the whole of the British Isles, even though the aristocracies of Scotland, Wales and Ireland have certain national differences. Of course, the starting-point in Scotland, Wales and Ireland comes later than the Tudors; not, in fact, until the great families of these countries became recognizably 'British'. In Scotland, this began to happen after James VI ascended the English throne as James I; in Wales, when Henry VIII imposed primogeniture on a people of largely princely descent whose lands had been repeatedly split up between brothers; and in Ireland, the process began with the late sixteenth-century 'Plantations'.

The great contemporary British families of medieval aristocratic descent would naturally have every right to object to such a partial view of history and it is only fair that they should be treated in a properly medieval context. but this is not the place for exhuming the many great names of the Middle Ages from what Lord Justice Crewe (in the De Vere claim to the Lord Great Chamberlainship) sonorously called 'the urns and sepulchres of mortality'. 'For where is Bohun, where is Mowbray, where is Mortimer, nay, which is more and most of all, where is Plantagenet?' intoned this seventeenth-century worthy. We are concerned here with the survivors.

Less than two dozen English peers of the present day are descended in the male line from ancestors who were peers in the Middle Ages. These are, of course, headed by the House of Howard, whose forebear, Sir John Howard, was made Duke of Norfolk in 1483. The title, which survives as the oldest dukedom outside the royal family, had previously been held by his mother's family, the Mowbrays, an historic medieval dynasty descended in the female line from Edward I's son, Thomas of Brotherton, Earl of Norfolk.

The Howards themselves had been modest landowners in East Anglia before the Mowbray marriage put them firmly on the map. The son of this union, John Howard, certainly had an eye for the main chance, ingratiating himself with Edward IV before becoming the indispensable side-kick of his brother Richard III; but it rather depends on which school of history you follow as to how to judge his career. As Constable of the Tower of London — a place that has loomed large in the history of the Howard family — at the time the 'little Princes' disappeared, Sir John has generally been implicated in their death and in the murky sequence of events that led to Richard III's accession to the throne. He was, literally, Richard's right-hand man when the new king sat upon the chair of state in Westminster Hall on 25 June 1483; three days later Sir John Howard was created Duke of Norfolk and Earl Marshal of England and at the coronation it was he who carried the crown and his son, Thomas, the sword of state.

Those who cast the hunchback king and his Howard henchman as the villains of the piece make particular play with the Dukedom of Norfolk itself. For one of the little Princes, the Duke of York, had received the Dukedom of Norfolk on account of his infant marriage to the senior Mowbray heiress and had thus stood between Sir John Howard and the family estates. The date of the Howard ducal creation has been duly taken by some theorists as a guideline to the timing of the little Princes' possible murder.

Theory, though, remains the essence of this great historical controversy and the case against Richard III and the 1st Duke of Norfolk must still be considered unproven. Recent research has tended to rehabilitate the character of that much maligned monarch and of his wily friend. Whatever the true story of their lives, their deaths occurred side by side at Bosworth, where the Duke stopped an arrow.

The Dukedom of Norfolk was forfeited on account of the 1st Duke's adherence to the House of York, but it was given back to Thomas, the 2nd Duke, after this endurable old campaigner distinguished himself in command of the army which defeated James IV of Scotland at Flodden Field in 1513. Thomas Howard exemplified the quality of pragmatic survival, which is the key factor in the story of so many great British families, managing to serve in his time both the Houses of York and Tudor. He was also the progenitor of a well-stocked dynasty which kept the House of Howard to the fore in history. His grandchildren, for instance, included two wives of Henry VIII: Anne Boleyn and Catherine Howard.

Just as the 1st Duke of Norfolk had been Richard III's right-hand man, so the 3rd Duke performed a similar role for Henry VIII until finally falling foul of that fearsome monarch after the execution of the second of the 3rd Duke's

The noble tomb of the 19th Earl of Arundel (1407–35) in
the Chapel at Arundel Castle, redolent of the ancestral
Catholic glory of the Fitzalans and the Howards. The
gallant Earl, over six feet tall and equally brilliant in
tournaments and real war, was known as 'the English
Achilles'.

two nieces to become queen. As the Howards fell from royal favour, the family of another of Henry's six wives, the Seymours, increased their influence. The Dukedom of Norfolk was forfeited again in 1546 when the scheming 3rd Duke and his brilliant son, the Earl of Surrey, were attainted of high treason. The poet Surrey, 'one of the brightest ornaments of the House of Howard', who introduced the Petrarchan sonnet to English literature, was discovered to have adhered to the Catholic religion and had apparently upset the Seymours by incorporating the royal arms into their heraldic achievement to which the Howards were entitled through their descent from the Mowbrays. He was executed for his pains and a week later his father, the 3rd Duke, was due to share the same fate, only to be saved from the scaffold by the death of Henry VIII. In the event, the 3rd Duke was able to die peacefully in bed in Norfolk, having had the Dukedom restored to him by Mary Tudor. His bed had been frequently occupied by 'that drab Bess Holland', who had been a washer in the nursery of the Duchess: a notorious liaison that caused a serious rift in the Howard family.

The Howards were in their element again in the early Elizabethan era. The Queen herself was a close cousin, being the daughter of Anne Boleyn, and her coronation was notable for the preponderance of Howards taking part in the proceedings. The 4th Duke of Norfolk (the poet Surrey's son), however, over-reached himself like many an 'over-mighty subject' before him. After plotting to become the husband of Mary Queen of Scots in the hope of securing the ultimate prize for the Howard family, the English Crown, he was executed in 1572. Thus, yet again and this time for nearly a hundred years, the Dukedom of Norfolk was forfeited.

And so it came to pass that there were no dukedoms in existence in England; for the Seymour Dukedom of Somerset had also been forfeited upon the fall of the Protector Somerset twenty years earlier. After being introduced into the English peerage in the fourteenth century, the title (derived from the Latin *dux*, 'leader'), up until the seventeenth century, tended only to be given to close relations of the sovereign. In the seventeenth century the ducal order enjoyed a remarkable resurgence—culminating in 1726 in the record of forty dukes outside the royal family. Since then, the number has diminished again and there are now only twenty-six non-royal dukes. George III endeavoured to revert to the medieval practice of only conferring dukedoms on members of the royal family, though there were in fact about half a dozen non-royal dukedoms created in the nineteenth century.

Aside from his intentions towards Mary Queen of Scots, the 4th Duke of Norfolk had been married three times. His first wife was the heiress of Henry Fitzalan, Earl of Arundel, and through their marriage the great Fitzalan estates passed to the Howards. These included what is now the principal seat of the Dukes of Norfolk, Arundel Castle in Sussex. The Castle, largely destroyed by the Parliamentarians in the Civil War, was to be grandly rebuilt

Van Dyck's portrait of Henry Percy, 9th Earl of
Northumberland (1564–1632). Known as the 'Wizard Earl'
on account of his scientific experiments and patronage of
mathematics, Lord Northumberland languished in the Tower
of London for sixteen years on suspicion of complicity in the
Gunpowder Plot.

in the 'Early English' style in the nineteenth century.

Apart from the estates, the Howards also gained the Earldom of Arundel. It was by this historic title that the successive heads of the family were known until the Dukedom of Norfolk was finally restored in 1660. Thus the early seventeenth-century 'Collecting Earl' of Arundel, who built up the collection of classical sculpture known as the 'Arundel Marbles', was the rightful Duke of Norfolk. So too was the Elizabethan Philip Howard, Earl of Arundel, who died in the Tower after suffering many years of imprisonment on account of his Catholic beliefs. He was canonized in 1970 as one of the Forty English Martyrs.

The Howards of Norfolk are regarded as England's premier Catholic family, but it cannot be said that their Catholicism has been unbroken. For example, the 4th Duke, despite his intrigues with the Catholic Mary Stuart, was a lifelong Protestant and his son, Saint Philip Howard, was a Catholic not by birth but by conversion. During the course of the seventeenth and eighteenth centuries, several members of the family 'conformed' to Protestantism, notably the raffish 11th Duke, known as the 'Jockey'.

This nickname probably owed more to the 11th Duke's addiction to the Turf than to the precedent of his ancestor, the 1st Duke (whose own sobriquet was a corruption of 'Jack'). 'Jockey' was a particular crony of 'Prinny', the future George IV. Together, according to a contemporary observer, they 'first established the later hours of dining — their dinner being a kind of Greek symposium, with Bacchus as the centre god'. The 'Jockey' is said to have formed a particular friendship with a neighbouring landowner in Cumberland (the Howard estates have been remarkably widespread), Mr Hudleston of Hutton John, for the reason that, when they drank together, the Duke first lost the use of his legs and Mr Hudleston the use of his voice. This meant that Mr Hudleston could get up and ring the bell for the servant, and the Duke, from his chair, could order more wine. Like the Prince Regent, the bibulous Duke was no fool, though. Almost a republican by political persuasion, he named his farms in honour of the American revolutionary leaders and their victories.

The Victorian 14th Duke, like Saint Philip Howard, was brought up as a Protestant but became a Catholic after making the acquaintance of contemporary French Catholic thinkers such as Montalembert. His son, the 15th Duke, was very much the leading Catholic layman of his time and he helped Newman to become a Cardinal. It was said of this Duke that 'he can hardly have known what it was to have an enemy', and he was mistaken, like several British aristocrats, for one of his own gardeners on account of his habitually shabby clothes. One haughty lady at a station once ordered him to carry her suitcase. 'Here my man,' she said, proffering the decrepit-looking individual a tip, 'I expect this is the first honest penny you have ever earned.' The Earl Marshal, pocketing the coin, murmured that indeed it was.

The 15th Duke's son by his first marriage was an invalid from birth; but by his second marriage to Lady Herries, a Baroness in her own right, he had another son, Bernard, who succeeded to the Dukedom at the age of eight.

The late (16th) Duke of Norfolk became a national figure more like the dukes of former times than those of the present. When he died in 1975 it was a major news event. Much of his fame was due to his masterly management of the ceremonial at great state occasions, for which the Dukes of Norfolk are responsible in their capacity as Earl Marshal, an office originally conferred on Thomas of Brotherton and held by the Mowbrays before passing to the Howards. He also made his mark as Her Majesty's Representative at Ascot, airing over the public-address system at one memorable race-meeting his uncompromising views about Lord Wigg and the Levy Board's plans for National Hunt racing on the course.

The present Duke has also played a leading part in Catholic affairs and was to the fore in the visit of Pope John Paul II to Britain in 1982. Miles Fitzalan-Howard started out as a soldier and reached the rank of Major-General before joining Flemings, the merchant bankers established by the grandfather of the creator of James Bond. It is a striking example of the happiness of the hereditary principle that such a suitable holder of the office of Earl Marshal should have succeeded to the title. Although a keen traditionalist, the present Duke lives very much in the modern world. One of his daughters is married to David Frost, the television tycoon; another, Marsha Fitzalan, the actress, is married to the leading young actor-producer Patrick Ryecart. The Norfolks divide their time between Arundel, a modest house near the river at Henley, and the amazing Gothic pile of Carlton Towers in Yorkshire. The Duke inherited the latter from his mother, the last of the Stapletons and eleventh holder of the Barony of Beaumont.

Four other peers are Howards of the Norfolk family, including the Earl of Suffolk and Berkshire and the Earl of Carlisle. Both these particular branches are descended from younger sons of the 4th Duke of Norfolk. The present Lord Carlisle, a land agent, is seated at Naworth Castle in Cumberland, Vanbrugh's palatial Castle Howard, which was built by the 3rd Earl, having passed to a junior line of the family descended from the 9th Earl. Lord Howard of Henderskelfe, proprietor of its vast Yorkshire estate until his death in 1985, was an appropriately eighteenth-century sort of polymath; a man of no little substance who combined the chairmanship of the BBC with the presidency of the Historic Houses Association, that effective heritage lobby. Even he came to refer to his home as 'Brideshead', following the famous television series filmed at Castle Howard which is now occupied by his son Simon.

Lord Suffolk still maintains an apartment in one of the towers of the Jacobean Charlton Park in Wiltshire, which has now been restored and converted by Christopher Buxton, the pioneer of multiple occupation as a means of survival for country houses. The present Earl's father, a colourful and highly courageous figure, was blown up when engaged in bomb disposal work in the last war, and awarded a posthumous George Cross. A television series was made of his life, romantically entitled *The Dragon's Opponent*. Before being raised to an earldom, the 1st Earl of Suffolk, whose wife built the prodigious house at Charlton, was made a 'baron by writ' as Lord Howard de Walden. The title later passed out of the Suffolk family by way of heiresses and the present Lord Howard de Walden, a prominent figure on the Turf and thrice Senior Steward of the Jockey Club, has only a female descent from the Howards. His prize possessions are the Marylebone estates in London which his family inherited from the eccentric 5th Duke of Portland.

A much older and more historic barony by writ associated with the Howards is that of Mowbray (dating from 1283), which the first Howard Duke of Norfolk inherited through his mother. The title was held by subsequent Dukes of Norfolk until the death of the childless 9th Duke in 1777, when it fell into abeyance between his nieces, one of whom had married another long-established Catholic peer, the 16th Lord Stourton. The Mowbray Barony was called out of abeyance a century ago and is now held by Lord Mowbray, Segrave and Stourton, familiar for his black eye-patch. As well as being one of the select company of peers descended in the male line from the medieval English peerage — his Stourton ancestor having been raised to the peerage in 1448 — this genial figure and loyal Tory servant in the House of Lords enjoys, as Lord Mowbray, the proud boast of being Premier Baron of England.

There are in fact numerous medieval English baronies still in existence and most of them were created by 'writ of summons' which differed from the more usual mode of creation by 'letters patent' in not specifying how the peerage should descend. This means that if the holder of one of these baronies has no son, the title can descend to his daughter and on to her heirs, male or female. But if he has more than one daughter, the title is deemed to be 'in abeyance' until 'called out' by the sovereign in favour of one of the sisters or her heir.

Thus the survival of these ancient baronies by writ is not particularly remarkable since they can pass indefinitely through the female line, and they have mostly passed in this way to families quite unconnected with their original holders. The Barony of de Ros, originally created in 1264 by Simon de Montfort during his usurpation of Henry III's government, passed in the fifteenth century to Sir George Manners, ancestor of the Duke of Rutland, who still owns some of the lands of the medieval Lords de Ros and their castle of Belvoir in Leicestershire. The Barony itself, however, passed out of the Manners family by way of an heiress in the seventeenth century.

Of the historic medieval Houses still represented in the present-day peerage in the male line, such as those of Manners, Vernon, Hastings,

The 12th Earl of Derby (1752–1834), noted for his excessively
large head and his passion for horse-racing and cock-fighting.

Lumley, Sackville, Clifford, Courtenay, Willoughby and Nevill (descended from an uncle of that archetypal 'over-mighty subject', 'Warwick the Kingmaker', otherwise Richard Nevill), only three can claim a medieval title above the rank of baron. These are the Howards, Dukes of Norfolk; the Talbots, Earls of Shrewsbury and the Stanleys, Earls of Derby. Like so many other peers of ancient lineage, Lord Shrewsbury no longer possesses an ancestral seat — the ruined Alton Towers has become Britain's answer to Disneyland — but the Earl of Derby still owns the enormously valuable estate of Knowsley in Lancashire, almost encircled by motorways and the industrial sprawl of Liverpool.

In Lancashire the Stanleys occupy the position of local royalty — 'God save the Earl of Derby and the King!' was the loyal Lancastrian's toast. They also used to enjoy the sovereign rights over the Isle of Man, which were granted to Sir John Stanley in 1406. Sir John's grandson became Lord Stanley fifty years later, and in 1485 the 2nd Lord Stanley was made Earl of Derby.

The splendidly Anglo-Saxon title of 'earl' is the equivalent of the foreign 'count'. An earl's wife is, of course, a countess and earls originally governed territories which were thus known as counties. Long after earls had ceased to be territorial administrators, it continued to be customary for them to take their titles from counties or county towns.

Unlike the Howards, the Stanleys chose the right side at Bosworth, for the 2nd Lord Stanley was the stepfather of none other than the victorious Henry Tudor. Indeed, the crown was placed on the head of the new Henry VII on the Field that day by Lord Stanley, who had married, as his second wife, Margaret, the widow of Edmund Tudor, Earl of Richmond.

The Complete Peerage notes that the 1st Earl of Derby 'skilfully betrayed' the cause of Richard III who had previously appointed him Constable of England and a Knight of the Garter. The 3rd Earl also hardly lived up to the family motto of '*Sans Changer*' for, as one historian put it, 'under Edward VI he acted as a Commissioner for the advancement of the Reformation; under Mary he delivered Protestants to be burnt at the stake; under Elizabeth he hunted Catholics to the death'. In short, like the Howards and other great dynasties, the Stanleys knew on which side their bread was buttered. To the 3rd Earl's credit, it can be said that he was a generous host: with his death, observed Camden, 'the glory of hospitality seemed to fall asleep'.

The principal Stanley seat, Lathom House, was razed to the ground in the Civil War by the Roundheads. Earlier, Charlotte de la Trémoïlle, Countess of Derby, had heroically held out for the King against overwhelming Parliamentary forces for the whole of 1644. Her husband, the 7th Earl, was away fighting for the Cavaliers at the time; he too was to meet a cruel fate after the Battle of Worcester, when he was beheaded. The family moved to another Lancashire property, Knowsley, and slightly to the wings of the historical stage.

The 10th Earl of Derby harboured a grudge about Charles II's ingratitude to the Stanleys and had inscribed a tablet at Knowsley in 1732 recording that the monarch had 'refused a bill unanimously passed by both Houses of Parliament for restoring to the family the estates' lost by loyalty to his cause. Upon the death of the 10th Earl, the Earldom and the Lancashire estates passed to a junior branch of the Stanleys, and the sovereignty of the Isle of Man went, by way of an heiress, to the Scottish Duke of Atholl.

The 12th Earl — whose second wife, the actress Elizabeth Farren, was painted by Lawrence — achieved immortality by instituting the great race at Epsom. And so the Stanleys came back into the limelight with successive earls distinguished for their learning, political activities and patronage of the arts, as well as in sport. The 14th Earl, a poet and a scholar, was described as 'the cleverest young man of his day' and he refused the throne of Greece with the inquiry 'Don't they know I am going to be Earl of Derby?'. (Certainly a more solid prospect, it might be thought.) He also later refused a dukedom. This great Victorian personage went on to become thrice Prime Minister; and the next three Earls of Derby all served in the Cabinet.

The third of them was the famous 17th Earl of Derby, the stout and benevolent 'King of Lancashire' who died in 1948 — one of the last examples of a peer who, regardless of his personal achievement, was a great national figure through his position and his high sense of duty. As well as being a long-serving statesman, the 17th Earl was a formidable figure on the Turf, sporting the familiar racing colours of black silks and white cap. The political tradition of the Stanleys was carried on by his two sons, Lord Stanley (who did not live to suceed to the Earldom) and Oliver Stanley, Secretary of State for the Colonies.

The 17th Earl of Derby's grandson, the childless present Earl, is a former Lord-Lieutenant of the county and now lives in a substantial neo-Georgian House (built with ten servants' bedrooms in the 1960s) in the great park at Knowsley which is a beautiful oasis in the desert of south Lancashire. The main house is partly let to the local police. It has largely been reconstructed in this century as a neo-Georgian palace by the 17th Earl and his grandson: 'It is more of a restoration to what never existed, to use an Irishism, than an old house', explained the former. The heir to the title is the present Earl's nephew, Edward Stanley, an officer in the Grenadier Guards and a godson of the late Duke of Windsor.

A junior branch of the Stanleys, descended from the 1st Lord Stanley's third son, is represented in the peerage by Lord Sheffield, who also holds the better-known nineteenth-century title of Lord Stanley of Alderley. In the Victorian age and afterwards, this branch produced many clever and eccentric personalities. The 2nd Lord Stanley of Alderley was a particular chum of Palmerston's, serving in all his Cabinets; his wife was a pioneer of women's education and founded Girton. His brother was Bishop of Norwich, whose son in turn was Arthur Stanley, the eminent Dean of Westminster and biographer of Matthew Arnold.

The 2nd Lord Stanley of Alderley's own children presented a broad range of religious persuasions. Algernon, a Catholic convert, became a titular bishop in 1903, spending most of his time in Rome ('Holy Mother Church sees to it that we don't starve', he said); whereas Henry, the 3rd Baron, became a Muslim. His nephew, Bertrand Russell, described the latter as 'the greatest bore I ever knew'. At his funeral which took place at the family seat of Alderley in Cheshire (now demolished), another nephew doffed his hat at the moment of committal, prompting Monsignor Stanley to say: 'Not your hat, you fool, your boots'.

Debunkers of the antiquity of the great British families often try to make play with the novelty of many of the peerage titles without grasping the fact that the dynasties holding them are, on the whole remarkably long established. Another popular belief is that peers bearing historic medieval surnames have mostly inherited them through heiresses and are, in the male line, of less august descent. There are, indeed, certain instances of this and the classic one, always cited with relish, concerns the Duke of Northumberland. Although he bears the unbeatably historic surname of Percy, he is descended from the medieval Percys only in the female line and is by male descent — wait for it — a Smithson.

In all fairness, the Duke's Smithson ancestors are perfectly acceptable by normal English aristocratic standards: solid Yorkshire gentry, who obtained a baronetcy — a sort of hereditary order of knighthood started by James I — in 1660. But the contrast between Percy with its evocations of that great medieval hero Harry Hotspur and the homely Smithson is such as to provide an unfailing source of ammunition and amusement. The contrast caused some raising of eyebrows in 1750 when Sir Hugh Smithson, 4th Baronet, whose wife was the eventual heiress of the extinct Percy Earls of Northumberland, changed his name to Percy and inherited a new Northumberland earldom (which had been conferred on his father-in-law with remainder to him). Seven years later he solicited and was given the Garter — 'the first Smithson to have it' as George II is said to have unkindly remarked — and in 1766 the ambitious Sir Hugh Smithson was made Duke of Northumberland and Earl Percy.

Ironically the name Sir Hugh was so keen to divest himself of — Smithson — became famous through the scholarship and munificence of his bastard son. For James Smithson, the scientist after whom the 'Smithsonite' carbonite of zinc is named, was a by-blow of this new Duke of Northumberland. A radical of republican persuasion, Smithson left a sizeable part of his considerable fortune 'to the United States of America, to be found at Washington, under the name of the Smithsonian Institution, an establishment for the increase and diffusion of knowledge among men'.

'The King of Lancashire': the redoubtable 17th Earl of
Derby photographed at Epsom on Derby Day, 1921.

The Percys of the present line have also been inclined towards scholarship and science, in this respect taking after the early seventeenth-century Earl of Northumberland who was known as the 'Wizard Earl' on account of his scientific experiments. Two Dukes of Northumberland have been Fellows of the Royal Society, and several have been Presidents of the Royal Institution. The present Duke has taken a particular interest in agricultural improvement and wildlife; his daughter Lady Julia is an architectural historian and his brother Lord Richard is Lecturer in Zoology at Newcastle University, where the Duke himself is Chancellor.

As well as his connections with scholarship and public life, the present Duke has more ducal connections than any other peer at the present time — when it is much less usual for dukes to marry the daughters of dukes than it was in days of yore. He himself married a duke's daughter; both his sisters married dukes; his mother was the daughter of a duke and so was his paternal grandmother.

A century ago, the pious 6th Duke of Northumberland was the largest landowner in England, with 186,000 acres, bringing in £176,000 a year. He had three country seats and until 1874 had owned Northumberland House, at Charing Cross, the last of the great Tudor and Jacobean palaces which lined the banks of the Thames upstream from Westminster. Some of its Adam furniture was removed to the sixteenth-century Syon House, down the river opposite Kew Gardens, which was originally a convent, passing to the Northumberlands by way of Henry VIII (whose corpse was worried by dogs here), Protector Somerset and James I.

The 1st Duke of Northumberland commissioned Robert Adam to create a superb series of state rooms at Syon which has splendid contents including Adam furniture and Rubens's 'Diana Returning from the Hunt'. The gardener 3rd Duke refaced the exterior in Bath stone and built the conservatory in the 1830s. Today there is a flourishing garden centre at Syon where the present Duke still lives when he is not at the mighty Alnwick Castle (now partly let as municipal offices), the medieval stronghold of the Percys in Northumberland. Alnwick was restored in the nineteenth century, to look even more 'medieval', by the architect Anthony Salvin.

Great British bastards are also not as numerous as popularly supposed; families in the peerage of august but illegitimate descent total not more than about twenty. Chief among them are the Somersets, Dukes of Beaufort and Lord Raglan, who, but for the illegitimacy of their early Tudor ancestor, the 1st Earl of Worcester, would rank higher than any family in the peerage, being, in fact, Plantagenets. They are descended in the direct male line from Edward III's son, the most 'over-mighty subject' of all, John of Gaunt. The 1st Earl of Worcester was the bastard of Henry Beaufort, 2nd Duke of Somerset, and took Somerset as his surname; his father was descended from John Beaufort, Earl of Somerset, one of John of Gaunt's children by

Catherine Swynford, children who were born before he married her but afterwards legitimated.

That staunch Cavalier, the 5th Earl of Worcester, was made Marquess of Worcester by Charles I as a reward for his loyalty. He devoted the greater part of his fortune to the Royalist cause and gallantly defended his castle at Raglan in Monmouthshire when it was besieged by the Roundheads. His son, the second Marquess, was a many-sided genius with a claim to have invented the steam-engine. After the Civil War, the 2nd Marquess's son abandoned the traditional Catholicism of his family, courted Cromwell and sat in the Rump Parliament as 'Mr Herbert' (Lord Herbert being his courtesy title). Although this rather spoilt the royal record of the family, as a means to an end it was successful, for he managed to recover the great estates in the Welsh Marches which the Roundheads had confiscated from his father. In any event, before the Restoration he made his peace with Charles II, who eventually created him Duke of Beaufort.

The 1st Duke of Beaufort later showed his loyalty to the deposed James II by refusing to take the oath of allegiance to William III. For the rest of his life he lived in retirement at Badminton in Gloucestershire which had taken the place of the battered Raglan Castle as the principal family seat. He lived there in princely style with a household of more than two hundred; his monument in the church attached to the house was executed by Grinling Gibbons who also did luscious carvings in the dining-room. William Kent remodelled Badminton in the 1740s, as well as designing the domed Worcester Lodge in the park, which is famous as the setting for the annual horse trials started by the present Duke in 1949.

The Victorian 8th Duke of Beaufort was one of the most likeable grandees of his time. He would purposely drive in his carriage through the poorest quarter of Bristol, believing that it gave pleasure to the people to see him go by. And indeed it seemed to, for the sight of his carriage brought them hurrying out on to the street, crying 'The Dook, the Dook!' He and his wife were devoted to one another, but this did not prevent him from having affairs with numerous other women.

The tastes of one of his younger sons, Lord Arthur Somerset, lay in a different direction; in 1889 he had to leave the country in the wake of the notorious Cleveland Street scandal, when he was found by the police in a homosexual brothel in London. A few years earlier, another of the 8th Duke's younger sons, Lord Henry Somerset, a promising young politician and a great friend of Disraeli's, was involved in a scandal of a similar nature when he was accused of homosexuality by his wife. He, too, went into exile, though nothing was actually proved against the poor man and he continued to be a Privy Councillor. The scandal caused his wife to be ostracized by society just as Lord Henry himself was, reputedly because Victorian ladies were not supposed to know about unnatural behaviour — let alone accuse their husbands of it. But it is said that the real reason was that people believed her accusations to be false. Sir Osbert Sitwell, his first cousin once removed, gave us a delightful picture of Lord Henry in his old age, when he lived in —

> . . . an elaborate and, taken in all, rather hideous little palace in Florence; a very tall Don Quixote in broad-trimmed hat and gold mono-grammed carpet slippers taking the air in the side-car of a motor-cycle through streets lined with an appreciative, indeed rocking, crowd.

Lord Henry's great-grandson, David Somerset, the art dealer who is married to the Marquess of Bath's elder daughter, succeeded to the Dukedom of Beaufort in 1984. The Beauforts' eldest son, the Marquess of Worcester, who is something of a rock singer, is married to Tracy Ward, the actress best known for her role in the television police series *C.A.T.S. Eyes*.

The late Duke, known as 'Master', was the doyen of the equestrian world and a legendary figure in the hunting field. His nickname did not originate from the fact that he was a long-standing Master of the Beaufort Hunt nor from his Mastership of the Horse to three sovereigns, but went back to child-hood. When he was only eight, his father, the 9th Duke gave him his own pack of harriers, the Brecon.

Through his marriage to the niece of Queen Mary, the Duke was a member of the royal family, the younger members of whom are now congregating so densely in 'Beaufortshire'. The Duchess's majestic but not exactly rural-minded aunt spent the war years at Badminton, where Her Majesty's enthusiasm for salvaging scrap iron would result in harrows and other agricultural implements being brought in from the fields. When someone inquired of Mary Beaufort as to what part of the great house the old Queen had lived in, the Duchess replied: 'She lived in all of it'.

When a hunting accident in 1978 caused the Duke to retire from his record forty-two-year stint as Master of the Horse, the Queen commissioned a special portrait by Terence Cuneo showing him at Buckingham Palace with Her Majesty and Prince Philip looking on. This decorated the Duke's study together with a handsome Landseer of the 8th Duke and his family (plus the inevitable dogs and a pony) and some signed photographs of Basil Brush. The Duke was not amused when the boundary changes placed his house in the absurd new county of 'Avon' and some of his park in Gloucestershire. Sadly, his right to stop trains at Badminton Halt lapsed when the railways were nationalized after the last war.

The Beauforts' Welsh estates still run to over 40,000 acres (in addition to the Badminton acreage of 19,000) and the late Duke's cousin, Lord Raglan, lives not far from Raglan itself in the centre of the ancestral lands of the Somerset family which the 1st Duke of Beaufort deserted when he moved across the Severn. Lord Raglan descends from the unfortunate Crimean War

The Queen with the present dashing Duke of Beaufort at
the entrance to Badminton where the annual horse trials
are regularly attended by the royal family.

The Egyptologist Earl of Carnarvon and his associates,
including Howard Carter, outside the entrance to
Tutankhamun's tomb in 1923. Lord Carnarvon's death soon
afterwards from an infected mosquito bite helped to give
rise to the legend of 'Tutankhamun's Curse'.

general who was the youngest son of the 5th Duke of Beaufort. The little kingdom in the Welsh Marches came to the Somersets through the marriage of the 1st Earl of Worcester to an heiress of the Norman-Welsh House of Herbert.

The Herberts, who became Earls of Pembroke in 1468, are represented by several families in the peerage today. The present Earl of Pembroke and the Earl of Carnarvon are descended from a natural son of one of the fifteenth-century Earls of Pembroke. Sir William Herbert, 1st Earl of Pembroke of the present line, was a powerful figure under the Tudors to whom Henry VIII — the brother-in-law of his wife, who was a sister of Henry's last queen, Catherine Parr — granted the Abbey of Wilton, near Salisbury, which he transformed into a great Tudor house. The Roundhead 4th Earl of Pembroke gave Wilton its Inigo Jones front, making it one of the most beautiful country houses in England.

Even before that famous front — which contains the stupendous Double Cube room and looks out over the architect 9th Earl's charming Palladian bridge — had been conceived, Wilton had acquired a reputation all of its own. As the home of the Elizabethan 2nd Earl and his Countess, and of their son, the 3rd Earl, it was, in the words of John Aubrey, 'an academie as well as a palace'. The brilliant court of painters, musicians, engineers and poets included the Countess's brother, Sir Philip Sidney, and Shakespeare, who gave the first performance of *As You Like It* at Wilton. The bard described the 3rd Earl and his brother, the future 4th Earl, as 'incomparable'.

Wilton has been called the nursery of the English Renaissance, standing for the concept of the 'Complete Man'. This concept has indeed been personified by the Herberts themselves who have produced generals, statesmen and scholars down the generations. The late Earl of Pembroke was a distinguished connoisseur of the arts and his son, the present Earl, is a stylish figure in the film world, best known for unveiling the charms of Miss Koo Stark, Prince Andrew's sometime girlfriend, in *Emily*. The flamboyant David Herbert, the present Earl's uncle, lives in Tangier and wrote an amusing autobiography appropriately entitled *Second Son*.

Wilton is a popular showplace, but the Victorian pile of Highclere, seat of the Earls of Carnarvon, was not opened to the public by the late Earl even though that sportsman and *bon vivant* could not exactly be described as a shrinking violet. With his somewhat theatrically rakish manner, 'Porchy' Carnarvon proved an irresistible show-off on television, promoting his racy memoirs. Racing parlance was 'Porchy' Carnarvon's preferred mode of speech and his most celebrated *bon mot* was addressed to his old army friend, Sir 'Jock' Delves Broughton, when the Baronet was acquitted of the murder in Kenya of the 22nd Earl of Erroll. 'Congratulations', went the telegram (later framed at White's Club), 'on winning a neck cleverly.' The present Earl is racing manager to the Queen.

An early photograph, taken in 1856, showing the Crimean
War general Lord Raglan discussing tactics with Turkey's
Omar Pasha and General Pelissier.

This branch of the Herberts descends from a grandson of the 8th Earl of Pembroke, who inherited the large Highclere estate on the borders of Hampshire and Berkshire and was made Earl of Carnarvon in 1793. The present Earl's grandfather was the man behind the discovery of the tomb of Tutankhamun and his death soon afterwards of blood poisoning from an infected mosquito bite helped give rise to the legend of 'Tutankhamun's Curse'.

The Egyptologist Earl's half-brother, the politician Aubrey Herbert, was an expert on Ottoman affairs and a great friend of the Albanian nation. His son, the late Auberon Herbert, followed his father's tradition in championing oppressed peoples behind the Iron Curtain. One of Aubrey Herbert's daughters married Evelyn Waugh, whose own favourite daughter, Margaret FitzHerbert, was the author of a biography of her colourful grandfather.

Outside the peerage, another great Welsh landowning family, the Williams-Wynn Baronets can claim medieval origins and it has been estimated that the ancient aristocracy of Wales—*bonheddig*, or 'men with pedigrees', whose princely descent was unimpeachable—accounted for three-quarters of the population. The Throckmorton baronets of Coughton in Warwickshire are a classic example of an 'ocf' (old Catholic family).

Pride of place among the untitled great British medieval families must go to the once illustrious Yorkshire Catholic House of Scrope. Several Scropes feature in Shakespeare's plays, notably Richard III's powerful but ill-fated favourite, William Scrope, Earl of Wiltshire, who had 'the realm in farm'. Though far from 'middle class' as one of them was recently heard to claim, the Scropes' claims to greatness may have receded but in their time have held two baronies, two earldoms, and the sovereignty of the Isle of Man, as well as producing an Archbishop, two Bishops, a Lord Chancellor, four High Treasurers and two Chief Justices.

Some two dozen or more other untitled dynasties of distinction can claim medieval foundations, such as the Giffards of Chillington in Staffordshire (another Catholic family) and the Dymokes of Scrivelsby in Lincolnshire. However, the size of the estates in most of these squirearchical families places them among the lesser aristocracy rather than the greater, for all their worthily proud pedigrees.

While still discussing the untitled families, though, we can end this chapter with an historic dynasty that unquestionably included 'over-mighty subjects', the Berkeleys of Berkeley Castle. The ancient estates of this noble House are now owned by an untitled branch of the family who inherited the castle on the death of the last Earl of Berkeley forty years ago (when the senior male line became extinct and the Barony of Berkeley passed to the female line). The heir to the estates in 1942, the present owner's father, was in fact a thirteenth cousin of the late Earl's for their connection went back as far as the fifteenth century. The present Mr Berkeley is Master of the Berkeley Hunt, familiar for its yellow coats; it is said that in the eighteenth century the Berkeleys could hunt on their own land all the way to London (where, incidentally, the Cockey epithet of 'berk' commemorates the Hunt).

Berkeley Castle was granted in 1153 to Robert FitzHardinge, whose grandson, Robert de Berkeley, sided with the rebellious barons against King John. Its notorious claim to fame is as the scene for the barbaric murder of Edward II when Sir John Mautravers and Sir John Gurney, the custodians of the castle in the convenient temporary absence of Thomas, Lord Berkeley, ordered a red-hot spit to be thrust into the wretched monarch's bowels. As Gray wrote:

> The shrieks of death thro' Berkeley's roof that ring —
> Shrieks of an agonising king.

CHAPTER III

NEW MEN

TUDOR TIMES

THE DISAPPEARANCE of many of the old magnates during the cataclysmic Wars of the Roses was a contributing factor to the Agrarian Revolution. This began with the break-up of the feudal system and ended under the Tudors with enclosures of common land and the distribution of the former monastic estates. A new class of magnates emerged, rich but less so than the great feudal lords, as well as a new class of smaller landed proprietors. Indeed there are still many families holding the same land which their forebears obtained in this revolution.

'Revolution' may perhaps be too strong a word, suggesting that the old aristocracy was overthrown and a new one took its place. In fact, for the most part, it was a case of some families of the 'old' aristocracy becoming richer at the expense of others, or at the expense of the monasteries.

Because the servants of the Tudor monarchy who were rewarded with monastic lands are popularly known as the 'new men', one is inclined to think of them as upstarts. It should be stressed, however, that the majority of them sprang from the medieval landed aristocracy. A survey of the peers whose ancestors first entered the peerage in Tudor, Stuart, and even Hanoverian, times shows that a surprisingly large number are descended in the male line from medieval knightly families. Even the treacherous and malodorous Lord Rich (the man who perjured himself at the trial of Thomas More), generally regarded as one of the most plebeian of the 'new men', could trace his pedigree back to a great-grandfather who was Sheriff of London in 1441.

It was unusual for the Tudor 'new men' to be made peers, like the aptly named Rich. Most of them had to be content with knighthoods, though peerages were to be liberally bestowed on their descendants in the seventeenth century and later. The Tudors were reluctant to add to the numbers of the peerage which had dwindled to only fifty or so after the Wars of the Roses. This was part of the policy of keeping the aristocracy in order. The new wealthy magnates were tied to the monarchy by gratitude; as lords they might have got above themselves.

Queen Elizabeth did more than just keep the aristocracy in order; she turned it into the chief instrument of her rule, making the country gentlemen

William Cecil, 1st Lord Burghley, Queen Elizabeth's
shrewd and devoted chief minister, who built the great
Renaissance palace of Burghley in Northamptonshire.

work for her as rural administrators. Thus the landowners took on their familiar role as unpaid public servants, a role which they kept until recent times (and even now, after they have been shorn of their power, they maintain this tradition of service by working free for the community in many different ways). The traditional relationship between squire and parson also originated under the Tudors. It was the Reformation which produced the phenomenon — now so familiar, but then novel — of the squire attending the village church, reading the lesson and sitting in his family pew, with the royal arms giving official sanction to the proceedings.

The commercial expansion during the Elizabethan period and the growing wealth of the City of London also had a significant effect on the great families. The landed aristocrats competed with each other for the hands of the rich merchants' daughters for their eldest sons and encouraged their younger sons to take up mercantile careers. The landowners themselves were not averse to cashing in on the industrial potentialities of their neighbourhood: they smelted iron in the Weald of Kent and mined tin in Cornwall. The old medieval knightly family of Savile (later Earls of Mexborough), for instance, made money in the Yorkshire woollen industry. There are many surviving great British families whose ancestors were landowners in the Middle Ages, merchants in the Tudor period and landowners again after that. This robust Elizabethan alliance between the landowners and the merchants has endured to the present day, even though certain sections of the Victorian aristocracy may have had that proverbial distaste for 'trade' which has given rise to so many myths and misunderstandings.

Being so prosperous, the Tudor landowners built themselves many new country houses, ranging in size from palaces of Renaissance splendour — the Burghleys and Longleats and Wollatons — down to the modest and comfortable manor houses of the lesser gentry. Since the Tudors gave England an internal peace and security such as she had never previously enjoyed, these houses were, for the first time, unfortified. This is another instance of how the Tudor aristocracy differed from their predecessors and resembled those who came after them: instead of sheltering behind castle walls, they lived in pleasant and civilized houses with large windows overlooking garden and park and the surrounding countryside.

Of the small numbers of existing peerages of Tudor origin, almost half were held by families who cannot properly be described as 'new men' because they came of medieval knightly stock. Such families as the Seymours, Paulets, Comptons and Devereuxs fall into this category. The Seymours hold the highest-ranking Tudor peerage, the Dukedom of Somerset, conferred on that arch-rival of the Howards, the Protector Somerset, in 1547. The principal family estates, including the old royal forest of Savernake, passed to an heiress in the seventeenth century. A junior branch of the Seymours, however, became Marquesses of Hertford and still own the estate of Ragley

The drawing room at Arundel Castle, Sussex, the medieval
Fitzalan stronghold which passed by marriage into the Howards,
Dukes of Norfolk in the sixteenth century. The castle was largely
rebuilt at the end of the nineteenth century in the 'Early English'
revival style by the 15th Duke.

Simon Howard of Castle Howard, Yorkshire, Vanbrugh's sublime
Baroque palace and the location for the television series *Brideshead Revisited*.

The 1st Duke of Beaufort, who lived in princely state at
Badminton, Gloucestershire, painted with his Duchess and
their children by S Brown in 1685.

The most famous seventeenth-century interior in Britain: the Double
Cube Room (60 × 30 × 30 feet) at Wilton House, Wiltshire,
designed for the 4th Earl of Pembroke by the seventy-six-year-old Inigo
Jones and his son-in-law John Webb at the end of the 1640s,
after the previous interior had been gutted by fire.

The 4th Earl of Pembroke and his family at Wilton by Van Dyck.

The present Earl of Pembroke—a film and television director
during the week, stately home owner at the weekend—
photographed at his family seat of Wilton in Wiltshire,
arguably the most beautiful country house in England.

SERO, SED SERIO.

Robert Cecil, 1st Earl of Salisbury, the wily little
hunchback who succeeded his father William as Queen
Elizabeth's chief minister and continued in that office
under James I. He built the splendid Jacobean mansion of
Hatfield adjoining an old royal palace.

in Warwickshire, with its vast Caroline and Georgian mansion which the present Lord Hertford has courageously fought to maintain.

Curiously enough, the title marquess—deriving from *marchio*, a governor of 'marches' or border territories—has somehow never been very popular in Britain. 'The name of Marquess is a strange name in this realm', protested John Beaufort, Marquess of Dorset, on whom Richard II conferred a Marquessate in 1397, having first introduced the title of marquess into the English peerage in 1385. It has seldom been conferred except on great magnates and the result is that there are only thirty-seven marquesses at the present time.

The Paulets hold the senior English Marquessate, that of Winchester, conferred on their ancestor who served Edward VI, Mary Tudor and Elizabeth I as Lord Treasurer. When asked how he had contrived this remarkable record, the 1st Marquess of Winchester is said to have replied 'By being a willow, not as an oak'. Most of the family estates eventually passed to the Orde-Powletts, Lord Bolton, and the present Marquess lives in Zimbabwe. The Comptons of the dazzling pink-bricked Compton Wynyates in Warwickshire stepped up the ladder of the peerage more gradually, becoming Marquesses of Northampton in the early nineteenth century.

Like the marquessate, the title of viscount was not initially popular in Britain and the majority of the 130 or so existing viscountcies date from as late as the first half of the present century, when the title was particularly favoured by retiring Cabinet ministers. The premier Viscount of England is Viscount Hereford, a title created in 1550 for the Devereux family. He is a collateral descendant of Queen Elizabeth's unreliable, if unlucky, favourite, the 2nd Earl of Essex. Like the Seymours, Paulets and Comptons, the Devereuxs can trace their ancestry back to knightly landowners in medieval times.

Of the great families who descend from Tudor 'new men', the best known are the Cecils, Marquesses of Salisbury and Exeter, descended from Elizabeth I's Minister, William Cecil. Their ancestors were small gentry in the Welsh Marches, called Sysilt (hence the correct pronunciation of the surname as 'Sissel'). William Cecil's devoted service to the Queen brought him great wealth but no higher rank than a Barony as Lord Burghley. He took the title from Burghley House in Northamptonshire—now absurdly placed in modern Cambridgeshire—the great Renaissance palace which he built for himself and which has been the seat of his descendants down to the present day.

A shrewd and foxy operator, William Cecil was trained as a lawyer. Although he ended up as Queen Elizabeth's leading minister for forty years, his path to the top was somewhat hazardous. He first came to prominence as a protégé of the Duke of Somerset, but lost his legal offices on the Protector's fall in 1549. Switching his allegiance to the Duke of Northumberland landed Cecil in hot water over the unhappy affair of Lady Jane Grey. Under duress

'Salisbury Sisyphus' by Sir John Tenniel. The Victorian Prime
Minister, the 3rd Marquess of Salisbury, wrestles with the
age-old Irish problem.

The Olympic gold medallist Lord Burghley (*right*) — later
6th Marquess of Exeter — *en route* for America in 1925 with
his fellow athlete AR Perritt.

from Northumberland and the boy king, Edward VI, Cecil was one of the signatories to the letters patent settling the crown on the nine-days' queen. However, he managed to make his peace with Mary Tudor who accepted his word as 'an honest man'. Again, when Elizabeth came to the throne, she was in no doubt as to Cecil's worth. 'This judgment I have of you', she told him, 'that you will not be corrupted by any manner of gift and that you will be faithful to the State and that, without respect of my private will, you will give me that counsel which you think best'.

History has tended to take a less sympathetic view of the founding father of the Cecils. He has been described simply as a considerable statesman and a very uninteresting man. Lord Macaulay wrote that 'He was cautious, sober, minute, astute, something of the Polonius type, and had a passion for placing everything on record'. In this historian's view, William Cecil 'had a cool temper, a sound judgement, great power of application, and a constant eye to the main chance'. One cannot agree, though, with Macaulay's harsh judgement that 'He can hardly be called a great man'. After all, Queen Elizabeth said that 'No prince in Europe hath such a counsellor as I have in mine'.

When William Cecil died in 1598 he was succeeded as Minister by his younger son Robert Cecil, who continued in office under James I until his own death 'worn out with business' in 1612. A diminutive, unprepossessing figure, the second Cecil was variously called 'pygmy', 'elf' and 'little man' by Queen Elizabeth, while James I referred to him as 'his little beagle'. None could gainsay the beaver-like quality of his industry, though Bacon once told the King that Robert Cecil 'was fit to prevent affairs from getting worse, though he was not fit to make them better'.

Robert Cecil was only in fact William's second son and the Burghley estate in Northamptonshire passed to Thomas, the son by the first marriage. Robert acquired a fortune of his own, however, and built himself a grand Jacobean mansion adjoining the old royal palace at Hatfield in Hertfordshire which had been granted to him. Thus the two Cecil dynasties were founded and, appropriately enough, Robert was duly raised to the Earldom of Salisbury on the same day as his eldest brother was created Earl of Exeter.

In the late Georgian period the 10th Earl of Exeter and the 7th Earl of Salisbury both became Marquesses, a good example of how marquessates at this time were conferred on certain earls in recognition of their status rather than as a reward for their achievements, since neither was particularly distinguished. The 1st Marquess of Exeter was a landscape artist of somewhat limited talent and preferred to be known as 'Mr Jones'. He was to achieve immortality of a sort, though, in Tennyson's poem 'The Lord of Burleigh', through his romantic marriage to the peasant girl, Sarah Hoggins.

The wife of the 1st Marquess of Salisbury was a colourful character who used to gamble all night in the Long Gallery at Hatfield and take with her

The present chatelaine of Burghley, Lady Victoria Leatham
(daughter of the 6th Marquess of Exeter), who has brought the
house to life again with her knowledgeable presentation of
its unrivalled treasures.

when she drove out in her carriage a bag of golden guineas which she threw to the poor. A passionate rider to hounds, she was out hunting on the day she died aged eighty-five; almost blind and strapped to the saddle, she relied on a groom riding nearby to warn her of an impending fence. That night in 1835 she is thought to have knocked over a candle in her room; in any event, there was a conflagration in the west wing of Hatfield in which the redoubtable Marchioness perished.

After their prominence in Tudor days, the Cecils have rather gone into eclipse but in the reign of Queen Victoria they made a brilliant reappearance in the world of affairs. The 3rd Marquess of Salisbury, that archetypal Victorian paterfamilias with his beard and dignified presence, was Prime Minister three times and made Hatfield a great political meeting place. Among the many foreign potentates entertained there was the Shah of Persia who, being used to the idea of oriental nobles grabbing crowns, was so impressed by the grandeur of life at Hatfield that he warned Queen Victoria that her throne might be usurped by Lord Salisbury. In the best tradition of the high Victorian polymath, the great Marquess—like the Marquess in Galsworthy's *Forsyte Saga*—was also a chemist of considerable distinction and, despite the risks of another fire, in 1881 installed electric light at Hatfield. It was the first private house to be so equipped; an indoor telephone system was already operational.

The 3rd Marquess of Salisbury's father, the 2nd Marquess, was something of a snob who regarded his daughter-in-law, Miss Alderson, the daughter of a judge, as socially beneath his son. Actually the Aldersons are a typical example of the British professional, clerical and service dynasties at their best. The marriage, one of many instances of the gap between the lesser and the greater aristocracy being bridged, was a triumphant success: Georgiana Alderson made an excellent Marchioness of Salisbury and an admirable Prime Minister's wife.

Three of the bearded Prime Minister's sons were also statesmen and the Salisbury Cecils have been a byword for political activity ever since. The late Marquess of Salisbury was perhaps the last great Tory diehard. 'Bobbety', as he was known, was very much the senior statesman of the Conservative party and played a key role in the 'consultation process' by which the Tories used to choose their leaders before the system was reformed in the mid-1960s. After the resignation of Sir Anthony Eden in 1957, Lord Salisbury memorably quizzed members of parliament as to their preferences between Macmillan and Butler: 'Which is it, Wab or Hawold?'

The present Marquess sat in the Commons for a short spell in his younger days. His eldest son followed in the political traditions of the Cecils, formerly representing a constituency in Dorset, the county where the family also own one of the loveliest of all English country houses and gardens, at Cranborne—from which place the heir takes his courtesy title. His brother

The great nineteenth-century collector, Sir Richard Wallace,
bastard son of the Marquess of Hertford, in the picture
gallery at Hertford House, London, shortly before his death
in 1890. His treasures now form the nucleus of the Wallace
Collection.

Richard was tragically killed in Rhodesia while reporting the troubles before independence was granted. The former capital, Salisbury, was named after the Prime Minister Marquess.

Apart from their political eminence, the Cecils have also produced two delightful writers: Lord David Cecil and, in an earlier generation, Algernon Cecil. Lord David, Goldsmiths' Professor of English Literature at Oxford, wrote among many other books, an engaging account of *The Cecils of Hatfield*. His son, the actor Jonathan Cecil, was surely born to play PG Wodehouse's Bertie Wooster.

The late Marquess of Exeter, the Olympic gold medallist, is one of the few Exeter Cecils to have emerged into the limelight. The character of the aristocratic hurdler in the film *Chariots of Fire* was loosely based on this famous figure, whose public appointments included a stint as Governor of Bermuda. The present Lord Exeter, the athlete's nephew, lives in a religious community in British Columbia. Burghley, celebrated for its famous art collection and Verrio's murals, as well as for its horse trials, is now owned by a trust set up by the late Marquess, and is energetically administered by the late Marquess's daughter, the feisty antiques buff, Lady Victoria Leatham, who has done much to reawaken the beauty of this fairy-tale treasure house.

One of the newest of the Tudor 'new men' was Henry VIII's Secretary of State, William, Lord Paget, about whose origins nothing is known for certain. There is a legend, though, that his forebears were nail manufacturers in Staffordshire, a county in which, after his rise to power, he was granted extensive monastery lands. It was said of him that 'His education was better than his birth; his knowledge higher than his education; his parts above his knowledge, and his experience above his parts'. He had a long plain face, a large nose, ginger hair and forked beard and is credited with the following axioms: 'Fly the courte. Speke little. Care less. Desire nothing. Never earnest. In answer cold. Learne to spare. Spend in measure. Care for home. Pray often. Live better. And dye well.'

This self-made Secretary of State is now represented in the peerage by his descendant through the female line, the Marquess of Anglesey, a military historian and chairman of the Historic Buildings Council for Wales. His eighteenth-century ancestors took the name of Paget on inheriting the Paget Barony and estates. The family seat, Plas Newydd, overlooking the Menai Strait, is now owned by the National Trust, but the present Marquess and his wife, the daughter of that sadly unread novelist Charles Morgan, still live in part of it. Lord Anglesey has likened his position there to that of 'the lucky howdah sitting on the white elephant's back'.

The present family of Paget produced many nineteenth-century generals and admirals, of whom the Earl of Uxbridge, who at the Battle of Waterloo lost a leg but gained the Marquessate of Anglesey, is the best known. 'By God, sir, I've lost my leg!' exclaimed the gallant Uxbridge that epic June day

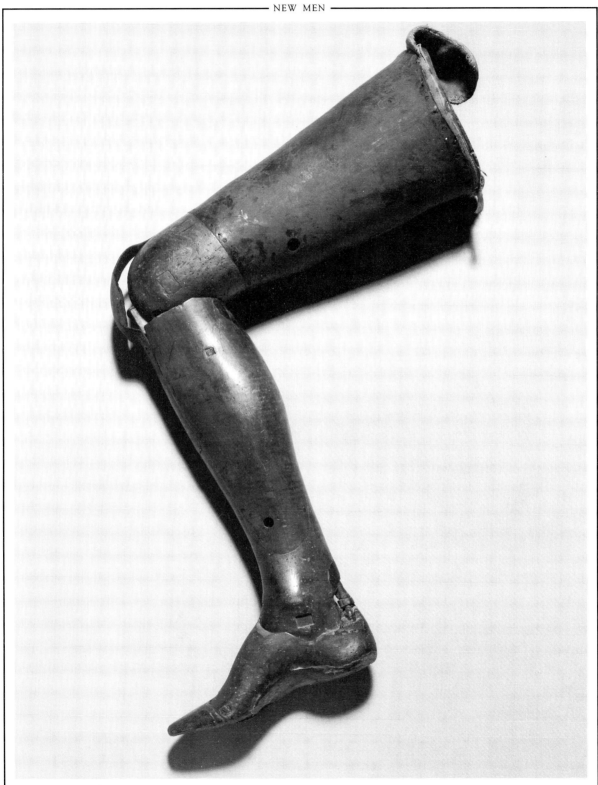

The wooden leg of the 1st Marquess of Anglesey who had
lost his natural limb at the Battle of Waterloo.

in 1815. The Duke of Wellington cast a cold eye on the damaged limb. 'By God, sir, so you have!' he said and carried on scrutinizing the Napoleonic retreat. The military Pagets proved such a formidable dynasty that they were almost regarded as a race apart; Queen Victoria once observed that there were men, women and Pagets.

The 5th Marquess of Anglesey, who succeeded at the age of twenty-three in 1898, was however of a very different stamp from his predecessors; in fact he is alleged not to have been a Paget at all, but a son of the French actor, Coquelin. His ruling passion was dressing up in bizarre and extravagant costumes. This outrageous character toured Europe with a theatrical company, putting on lavish productions in which he himself usually had a part; he also appeared in a solo act called the 'Butterfly Dance', which caused him to be known as the 'Dancing Marquess'. He ran a private theatre at Plas Newydd, which was later made into a dining-room by his cousin and successor, the present Marquess's father, and charmingly decorated in *trompe l'œil* by Rex Whistler.

The Dancing Marquess's performances, though quite well received by the critics, were ruinously expensive. He went bankrupt in 1904, a year before his death, owing a total of £255,969, mainly for jewels, of which he was a compulsive buyer. Indeed he desired his naked wife to be festooned with jewellery and the marriage does not appear to have been consummated. The Dancing Marquess was also a compulsive buyer of clothes; when his personal effects were auctioned, the sale of his wardrobe alone took a full three days.

As distinguished as the Cecils among the great families of Tudor origin are the Russells, descended from medieval wine merchants who had risen to being county gentry by the end of the fourteenth century. This great Whig dynasty's founding father, John Russell, had a varied career which began when he attached himself as interpreter to Archduke Philip on the latter's arrival in England near Weymouth in 1506. Accompanying the Archduke to Windsor, Russell was introduced to Henry VII, who appointed him a gentleman of the Privy Chamber. He later became a companion in arms of Henry VIII and was knighted in 1522 after the Battle of Morlaix in which action he lost not a leg, like Lord Uxbridge, but an eye. A string of important offices followed, such as Lord President of the Western Parts and Lord High Admiral, but it was in the field of diplomacy that he really made his mark.

A talent for diplomacy is one of the noted Russell traits. For instance, Sir John Russell's forceful interviews with Pope Clement VII were to be echoed down the centuries by the encounters of his Victorian descendant, Lord Odo Russell, with Pope Pius IX. The formidable Sir John was amply rewarded with a grant of monastery lands including Woburn Abbey in Bedfordshire; he was also created Baron Russell by Henry VIII and Earl of Bedford by Edward VI. Edmund Burke's slur that Russell was 'a prompt and greedy instrument of a levelling tyrant' is hardly justified when one considers that ten peers received

The 'Dancing Marquess' of Anglesey in one of his exotic
costumes.

larger grants than he did.

The early seventeenth-century Earls of Bedford greatly increased the family fortunes by draining the Fens. The 4th Earl rebuilt Woburn Abbey and developed Covent Garden, which had also been included in Sir John Russell's great haul of properties. The 4th Earl of Bedford's younger son John, a legendary dancer, may have been the model for Addison's Sir Roger de Coverley.

The great 'Bedford Level' scheme for the Fens was completed by the 5th Earl, who was created Duke of Bedford by William III. This creation was partly to honour the memory of his son, Lord Russell, who was regarded as a martyr to the Whig cause, having been executed after the Rye House Plot of 1683. The executed Lord Russell had contributed to the aggrandizement of the family in another way by marrying the heiress of the great Bloomsbury estate in London which made the Russells richer still.

The 1st Duke of Bedford began the Woburn tradition of entertaining paying guests: even his children had to cough up for their board and lodging. As for the 3rd Duke, Lady Mary Wortley Montagu wrote that his failure to consummate his marriage was due to his lack of 'a competent knowledge either of practical or speculative anatomy, and literally thinking fine ladies composed of lilies and roses'. His brother, the 4th Duke of Bedford, who rebuilt Woburn to the faintly dull designs of Flitcroft, seems to have been rather a put-upon character for he was hounded by his formidable grandmother-in-law, Sarah Duchess of Marlborough, as well as by the political rent-a-mob of the day. Once he had to suffer the indignity of being horse-whipped by a local attorney on Lichfield racecourse.

The 4th Duke of Bedford's bachelor son, Francis, had revolutionary leanings and was supposed to be a friend of Danton. He was also another noted agriculturalist and instigated the remodelling of Woburn by Henry Holland. Games, however, proved to be his undoing: a cricket bat at Westminster effected a rupture and then a tennis ball at Woburn finished him off. The botanist 6th Duke devoted himself to the pleasures of the table while his Duchess ('a red-faced vixen' in the view of her stepson) dallied with Landseer, half her age. The 6th Duke's first wife, Georgiana Byng, who died of consumption, brought a strain of despondency and melancholia into the Russell family.

'If one hadn't a few acres in London in these times of agricultural depression', remarked the Victorian 9th Duke, 'I don't know what one would do'. But his 'few acres in London' brought this shy and aloof Duke of Bedford much obloquy. He was accused of being indifferent to the lot of many of his tenants, who lived in dreadful slums. Yet, ironically, like so many of his forebears and like another bogey Duke of left-wing mythology, Sutherland of the 'Highland Clearances', Bedford was very much a progressive, an agricultural improver. He was also an advocate of cremation, building his own

I Russell Ld Privy Seale.   with one Eye

Holbein's sketch of Sir John Russell (1485–1554), who lost
his right eye in battle, received a generous helping of
monastery lands (including Woburn Abbey, Bedfordshire) and
was created Earl of Bedford by Edward VI.

crematorium which was inaugurated after he had ended his life by shooting himself in a fit of delirium during an illness.

The 9th Duke of Bedford's younger son, the 11th Duke, who died in 1940, became an even more remote figure than his father, living in lonely grandeur in the treasure-house of Woburn. Though by nature selfish, he devoted a considerable amount of his wealth to the underprivileged, largely through supporting the charitable activities of his wife, whose deafness made her as solitary a figure as he was. In her old age she took refuge in aviation, becoming famous as the 'Flying Duchess' and eventually was lost on a solo flight over the North Sea.

The eccentricity of the 11th Duke of Bedford and his Duchess took a different form in their son, the 12th Duke, a naturalist who devoted himself to wildlife and who quixotically advocated the cause of pacifism during the Second World War. However, he recalled the three previous Dukes in being something of a recluse. 'Spinach', as he was known, frequently exasperated his fellow peers in the House of Lords and one Lord Chancellor said he had 'a capacity to swallow any yarn which supported his jaundiced views'.

The present Duke of Bedford might well have been a recluse too, having inherited the Russell shyness. But he forced himself to face the glare of publicity as a pioneer of stately home showmanship in order to save Woburn which would otherwise have had to be sold owing to exceptionally heavy death duties. After the Abbey became a fun palace in 1954, the Duke felt obliged to start pronouncing it 'Woeburn' so as not to confuse his customers, but upsetting one of the 'smarty-pants' country-house cultists: 'It's Wooburn, Duke, *Woo*burn'.

This considerable enterprise is now run by the present Duke's son, the unassuming and serious-minded Marquess of Tavistock and his wife, the former Henrietta Tiarks, the last true 'Deb of the Year'. Educated at Harvard, Lord Tavistock is very much a modern businessman, whose City directorships include the Trafalgar House group — owners, incidentally of the Ritz, where he had the almost unique distinction of being born. He has said that 'Disneyland sets the standard for everything else' and that he regards the 1977 Neil Diamond concert at Woburn as 'one of the great occasions in the history of the house'.

Such views might not seem entirely to chime with his cousin, the philospher Bertrand Russell's definition of 'human excellence' as containing many elements 'associated with aristocracy such as fearlessness, independence of judgement, emancipation from the herd and leisurely culture'. The lecherous left-wing thinker was the 3rd Earl Russell, grandson of the Victorian Prime Minister, Lord John Russell. Lord John, a younger son of the 6th Duke of Bedford, was created Earl Russell in 1861. Young Bertie, incidentally, was very much alive in his grandfather's lifetime. It is remarkable to think that the eagle-like figure carried off to the cells from 'Ban the

Lord Odo Russell, a younger brother of the 9th Duke of
Bedford, was a prominent Victorian diplomatist, later
created Lord Ampthill.

Bomb' demonstrations in the 1960s could vividly remember a statesman born in 1792.

Another scion of the Russells, the Victorian diplomatist Lord Odo Russell, a younger brother of the 9th Duke of Bedford, was offered a peerage by Disraeli after the Berlin Conference of 1878. Lord Odo considered, however, in the best aristocratic traditions, that he could not become a peer without a suitable endowment. The theory used to be that a peerage should be supported by a suitable landed estate; the higher the rank, the broader the acreage required. So Russell asked his ducal brother to provide him with one. The Duke, a Liberal, refused to endow a peerage granted by a Conservative Prime Minister. And so the offer lapsed until it was repeated by Gladstone, when the Duke agreed to provide an endowment and Lord Odo duly became the 1st Lord Ampthill.

The Ampthill title became all too familiar in the present century owing to the publicity surrounding the sensational divorce case of John Russell (later 3rd Lord Ampthill) and the consequent paternity dispute which was a long-running treat for the prurient. Phrases such as 'Hunnish practices' and 'fecundatio ab extra' were splashed over the newspapers in 'The Baby in the Bath Case', giving rise to jokes about 'not wearing a nightdress because it might russell' — and worse. The affair concluded with the 3rd Baron's elder son, the film producer, Geoffrey Russell, establishing his right to the Barony over his halfbrother.

The 1st Lord Ampthill was just one of the many distinguished diplomatic Russells, the most recent of whom is Sir John Russell, former Ambassador to Brazil and Spain. His father, Russell Pasha, was the head of the Egyptian Police who did so much to combat the international drug traffic. Russell Pasha's daughter married Christopher Sykes, the author and biographer of Evelyn Waugh.

The subsequent rise of such Tudor 'new men' as the Russells, Cecils and Pagets to be dukes and marquesses illustrates the manner in which several of the great families in the first two ranks of the peerage have gradually achieved their present standing. In broad terms the dukes and marquesses of today can be said to represent the earls of the Tudors and Stuarts.

Of the great families outside the peerage that were founded in Tudor times, the territorial dynasty of Bacon deserves to be mentioned. The Bacons are collaterally descended from that eminent Tudor personage, Francis Bacon, essayist, philospher, Lord Chancellor and alleged author of Shakespeare's plays. The Norfolk worthy of the present time, Sir Nicholas Bacon, 14th (and 15th) Baronet, is Premier Baronet of England. The Baronetcy was conferred upon Francis Bacon's halfbrother in 1611 when the Order of the Baronetage was instituted by James I.

CHAPTER IV

ROYAL FAVOURITES

UNDER THE STUARTS

JAMES I AND THE OTHER Stuart monarchs greatly increased the numbers of the peerage, so that there are today about sixty peers whose families were first ennobled in the seventeenth century. By the outbreak of the Civil War the total number of peers had risen to 120. Many of the new peers were royal favourites and courtiers, for, as in the Tudor period, the aristocracy was now depending very much on royal favour.

The early Stuart age in England was notable for the high pitch of civilization achieved by the great families. It is epitomized by Van Dyck's portraits in the Double Cube Room at Wilton of the family of the 4th Earl of Pembroke, who with the help of Inigo Jones, made that loveliest of all English country houses what it is. Then this halcyon world of the 1630s was shattered by civil war.

Because of the amount of royal favourites and courtiers among the new peers, Charles I could count on as many as ninety supporters from among the peerage. The aristocracy as a whole was, however, divided between the Royalist and Roundhead camps, for the Civil War was not a class struggle, but a conflict over issues that were primarily religious. Outside the peerage many of the larger landowners tended to support parliament while the smaller squires — with the important exception of Cromwell himself, of course — were loyal to the King.

The result, characteristic of the story of the aristocracy, was that the great survived and the lesser perished. The Cavaliers who were ruined by the Civil War mainly came from the small gentry and their lands were often bought up by the territorial magnates, whether long established or parvenu. And, as is often the case in times of financial instability, the rich became richer and even more powerful.

After the Restoration, while the 'royal sufferers' sank without trace, the Roundhead profiteers were not generally penalized. Matters were improved for the great families in the course of the seventeenth century by the growth of the economy, principally due to overseas trade. Before too long things were more or less back to normal and aristocratic life flowed along once more at the stylish court of Charles II.

Without giving any support to the nonsensical theory that the peerage is largely composed of 'royal bastards', one has to concede that the seventeenth-century creations are dominated by the four Dukedoms provided by Charles II for his illegitimate sons. These were Buccleuch (a Scottish peerage created for the ill-fated Duke of Monmouth), out of Lucy Walters; Grafton, out of Barbara Villiers; St Albans, out of Nell Gwyn; and Richmond, out of Louise de Keroualle.

The 'House of Nell Gwyn' has been the least successful financially, so to speak. Although the 1st Duke of St Albans married the daughter and heiress of Aubrey de Vere, 20th and last Earl of Oxford, this illustrious match brought little else with it than the ancient blood of a family that had held an earldom since 1142. Sadly, the de Vere estates had been dissipated by the Elizabethan 17th Earl of Oxford, another of the alleged authors of Shakespeare's plays.

Several of the subsequent Dukes of St Albans married heiresses with more tangible assets, but none of them was rich by ducal standards. Indeed the Beauclerks, Dukes of St Albans, have never really possessed a family seat of any lasting significance. The present Duke has had to work for his living. After giving up his salaried job in the Central Office of Information when he succeeded the somewhat eccentric 'Obby' St Albans in 1964, he took on various company directorships. Perhaps the most interesting member of this ducal family has been Dr Johnson's friend, the convivial bibliophile Topham Beauclerk.

The other Caroline bastards have done pretty well for themselves. The line of Lucy Walters, the Dukes of Buccleuch, hold the enormous acreages of their maternal ancestors, the Scotts—Earls of Buccleuch, the Douglases—Dukes of Queensberry, and the Montagus—Dukes of Montagu, as well as the titles of the first two families. Although the glorious late seventeenth-century seat of the Montagus, Boughton, is in Northamptonshire, the three other principal Buccleuch mansions are in Scotland.

The Dukes of Richmond came into the vast estates of the Scottish Dukes of Gordon by marriage to that family's heiress. A hundred years ago, the 7th Duke of Richmond was credited with over 286,000 acres, and all but 17,000 of these were in Scotland. The Scottish inheritance has since been dispersed, but the Gordon-Lennox family is still in the driving seat at Goodwood in Sussex. The motor-racing metaphor is used advisedly as the present Duke is president of the British Automobile Racing Club and used to take the wheel in his younger days. The Goodwood estate is now actually run by the Duke's able heir, the Earl of March, a chartered accountant and a keen churchman.

It is fair to say that Goodwood is more famous for its 'glorious' racecourse than for its house which was bought as a hunting lodge by Charles II and Louise de Keroualle's son, the 1st Duke of Richmond. The 3rd Duke enlarged the house, landscaped the park and laid out the racecourse. Goodwood's fine collection of paintings includes the famous set of Canaletto's views of London. In addition to running Goodwood so smoothly, and his church commitments, Lord March has been a dedicated servant of the heritage lobby, working as treasurer and deputy president of the Historic Houses Association.

The HHA's patron is another illegitimate descendant of Charles II, Sir Hugh FitzRoy, the 11th Duke of Grafton. Irreverently known as the 'Duke of Preservation' he is a veritable 'Pooh-Bah' of the heritage world; his list of appointments and responsibilities in this field is impressive to a degree. The Graftons are friends of the present royal family and the Duchess is Mistress of the Robes. The family seat, Euston Hall in Suffolk, was originally built in the 1660s for the 1st Earl of Arlington, the first 'A' in Charles II's 'CABAL' and who always wore a black plaster on his scarred nose.

The 2nd Duke of Grafton also became the 3rd Earl of Arlington on the death of his mother, the black-plastered Earl's daughter. Dean Swift did not have a high opinion of the 2nd Duke — 'almost a slobberer, without one good quality' — but his public memorial remains the construction of the Marylebone Road in London. He also rebuilt the family seat in Suffolk. The 3rd Duke of Grafton was a distinguished statesman who was practically the Prime Minister when Pitt's health broke down in 1767. In the time of the 7th Duke of Grafton, a General, there was a major fire at Euston which severely reduced the size of the house and devastated the interior. The 7th Duke's eldest son, Lord Euston, is remembered for marrying a former circus artiste known as 'Flash Kate'. When he tried to divorce her, under paternal pressure, on the grounds of her bigamy, his suit failed as it was established that her other husband had already committed bigamy himself. Thus, Flash Kate's previous marriage was invalid and she really was the Countess of Euston after all. She did not, however, become Duchess of Grafton, dying some years before her husband, who himself predeceased his father.

Apart from Charles II's bastards, the principal servants of the Stuart monarchy are well represented among the peers of today. The Earls of Jersey and Clarendon are of the family of James I's egregious favourite, George Villiers, Duke of Buckingham. The latter earl can also claim a worthier servant of the Stuarts among his female-line ancestors — in Edward Hyde, the great Earl of Clarendon. Hyde's daughter, Anne, was the last English-woman — before Lady Diana Spencer — to marry an heir to the throne — the future James II. Lady Anne's father took a dim view of her secret match. The presumptuous strumpet, he felt, should be 'sent to the <u>Tower</u> and be cast into a Dungeon . . . an Act of Parliament should be immediately passed for the cutting off of her Head, to which He would not only give his Consent, but would very willingly be the first Man that should propose it'. (Something of a contrast, one might observe, between this statement and those of the obliging Earl Spencer after the 1981 royal wedding.)

Indeed all the letters of Charles II's 'CABAL' administration can be accounted for by present-day peers: Clifford by Lord Clifford of Chudleigh; Arlington (as we have seen) by the Duke of Grafton; Buckingham by the Earls of Jersey and Clarendon; Ashley by the Earl of Shaftesbury (whose more recent ancestor was the great nineteenth-century philanthropist); and Lauderdale is represented in the peerage in Scotland by the Earl of Lauderdale (father of the fragrant gossip columnist, Lady Olga Maitland).

At least a quarter of today's English peers whose families were first ennobled in Stuart times represent dynasties who were wealthy and powerful for at least two centuries before they were raised to the peerage. The families of these great county magnates include the Brudenells, Cholmondeleys, Townshends, Bridgemans, Stanhopes, Shirleys, Waldegraves, Digbys and Leighs. Chief among the important territorial dynasties raised to the peerage in Stuart times are, of course, the Cavendishs. James I made Sir William Cavendish a Baron in 1605 and later advanced him to the Earldom of Devonshire. The Dukedom was one of the many created by William III.

The Cavendishs had been seated at Cavendish Overhall in Suffolk since the fourteenth century, but rose to political power through the attachment of Sir William Cavendish (the 1st Earl of Devonshire's father) to the household of Cardinal Wolsey. This Sir William survived the fall of the Cardinal to become a firm favourite of Henry VIII and one of the protagonists of the Dissolution of the monasteries. He made one of the great matches of all time by marrying the mighty Derbyshire heiress, Bess of Hardwick.

Bess, who was married and widowed four times, ending up as the Countess of Shrewsbury, was an inveterate builder. Her most splendid achievement was Hardwick Hall, that stupendous house with its tall windows and the High Great Chamber described by Sir Sacheverell Sitwell as the 'finest room not only in England but in all Europe'. Hardwick is close by Chatsworth, 'the Palace of the Peak', where Bess carried on with the work on the Elizabethan house started by her husband.

Thus the 1st Earl of Devonshire inherited large estates from both his parents, and other heiresses brought more property into the family at subsequent periods. For instance, the eighteenth-century Prime Minister Duke of Devonshire married Charlotte, daughter of the amateur architect and patron of the arts, the Earl of Burlington and Cork. Through her the major part of the English and Irish lands of Richard Boyle, the great Earl of Cork, together with the estates of the Cliffords, Earls of Cumberland, came to the Devonshires. Through an heiress of the Comptons, who married the Prime Minister's youngest son, the family acquired the seemly seaside resort of Eastbourne.

Like the Russells, the Cavendishs are a great Whig dynasty which may help to explain why the present Duke of Devonshire has now joined the Social Democratic party. Indeed, the 4th Earl of Devonshire was one of the

Nell Gwyn, Charles II's earthy mistress, displays part
of her charms. She was the mother of Charles Beauclerk,
created Duke of St Albans in 1683.

original Whigs, much to the fore in the 'Glorious Revolution' which replaced James II by William III. The Russell Dukedom of Bedford and the Cavendish Dukedom of Devonshire were both created on 12 May in 1694 — a red-letter day for Whiggery — and the 2nd Duke of Devonshire married the sister of the 2nd Duke of Bedford.

The 5th Duke of Devonshire married the bewitching Lady Georgiana Spencer — 'the face without a frown' immortalized by Gainsborough. In Georgiana's time Devonshire House in Piccadilly became the centre of a brilliant cousinhood of Whig patricians. She caused a sensation by canvassing for Charles James Fox in the East End of London, giving a butcher a kiss to secure his vote. According to the memoirs of Sir Nathaniel Wraxall, her beauty consisted 'in the amenity and graces of her deportment, in her irresistible manners and the seduction of her society'. Her hair, Sir Nathaniel noted, was 'not without a tinge of red; and her face, though pleasing, yet had it not been illuminated by her mind, might have been considered ordinary'. She made the best of her looks through a remarkable feeling for fashion and her hair was piled high on her head below the famous ostrich plumes.

Georgiana's son was the 'Bachelor Duke', a scholar, connoisseur and horticulturist, who furthered the career of that early-Victorian genius, Sir Joseph Paxton, originally one of his gardeners at Chatsworth. The great scientist in the family, though, was Henry Cavendish, a grandson of the 2nd Duke, after whom the Cavendish Laboratory at Cambridge is named. Astronomer, mathematician and geologist, Cavendish's lasting claim to scientific fame was his demonstration in 1781 of the composition of water. His achievements were all the more remarkable in view of his extreme eccentricity. He gave his fellow human beings an extraordinarily wide berth and went to considerable lengths to avoid conversation. According to Lord Brougham, Cavendish 'uttered fewer words in the course of his life than any man who ever lived to fourscore years, not at all excepting the monks of La Trappe'.

The best-known politician in the Cavendish family was eccentric in a much more endearing way. 'Harty-Tarty', Marquess of Hartington (later the 8th Duke of Devonshire), the great Victorian statesman who dominated the Liberal party for many years, was engagingly devoid of personal ambition, thrice refusing the premiership. He took part in politics simply because he felt it to be his duty and, as he confessed, came 'to hate office'. This somnolent, bearded figure is said to have admitted to falling asleep in the middle of one of his own speeches.

'I don't know why it is', Harty-Tarty mused on one occasion, 'but whenever a man is caught cheating at cards the case is referred to me'. It has been suggested that PG Wodehouse might have had the old boy in mind when creating the character of the vague Earl of Emsworth (the proud possessor of that prize sow, the Empress of Blandings), for the 8th Duke of

Euston Hall, Suffolk, as it was before a bad fire in 1900.
Originally built for the 1st Earl of Arlington, it passed
to his daughter Isabella who married Charles II's bastard
by Barbara Villiers, the 1st Duke of Grafton, and remains
the seat of the present Duke.

The present Duchess of Devonshire at Chatsworth which
she has done so much to rejuvenate. One of the celebrated
Mitford sisterhood, 'Debo' too has become a highly individual
and amusing writer.

Devonshire was once heard to observe that his greatest moment was when his 'pig won first prize at Skipton Fair'. He did not marry until he was nearly sixty, carrying on affairs both with the courtesan called 'Skittles' (who was paid a pension by the family until she died in the 1920s) and with his eventual bride. The latter was the German-born Duchess of Manchester, who consequently became known as the 'Double Duchess'. Indifferent to his fabulous possessions, the 8th Duke's response to the enthusiasm of the Earl of Crawford as they walked through the state apartments of Chatsworth was to murmur, 'Rummy old place'.

Chatsworth was rebuilt and enlarged in the Baroque style towards the end of the seventeenth century and later. However, it was deserted for much of the eighteenth century and suffered a certain amount of nineteenth-century philistinism. Indeed, it can probably be said that it did not really come into its own until after the Second World War.

Although the late Duke's demise brought crippling death duties, the Devonshire family fortunes have been kept going by highly efficient management, the rise in property values and the sale of the odd picture. The stylishness of the family home owes much to the present Duchess, 'Debo', the youngest of the remorselessly publicized Mitford sisterhood — soon, no doubt to be portrayed on ice. Though she claims never to have read a book, the Duchess has herself produced a characteristically amusing account of the Cavendishs of Chatsworth. Her husband refutes the old jest about Debo waiting for the 'Duke of Right' to come along by pointing out that when they married he was, in fact, Lord Andrew Cavendish — the younger son. His elder brother, Lord Hartington, was killed in action in 1944.

The late Lord Hartington was married to Kathleen ('Kick'), the sister of John F Kennedy. Thus the American President was connected to his opposite number in Britain, Harold Macmillan, whose wife was Lady Dorothy Cavendish, the present Duke's aunt. It was Mr Macmillan, in his last administration, who appointed the present Duke to ministerial posts at the Commonwealth Relations Office. The present Duke's elder sister, Lady Elizabeth Cavendish, companion of the late Sir John Betjeman, the former Poet Laureate, is a lady-in-waiting to Princess Margaret, to whom she introduced the latter's future husband, Antony Armstrong-Jones.

The Kennedys are not the only well-known American family linked by marriage to the Devonshires, for the present Duke's uncle, Lord Charles Cavendish, married the dancer and singer, Adele Astaire, sister of the immortal Fred. Until her death, Miss Astaire used to stay every year in the Devonshires' Irish seat, Lismore Castle in County Waterford, where she had lived with her husband for the dozen years before his death in 1944.

Lismore was acquired in the late sixteenth century by Sir Walter Raleigh, who sold it in 1602 to Richard Boyle, the penniless settler who ended up as the Earl of Cork and one of the richest men in the British Isles. The bachelor

Duke of Devonshire grew very attached to the castle his grandfather had inherited from the Boyles and brought his right-hand man, Sir Joseph Paxton, over to remodel it. The garden overlooking the Blackwater river is open to the public.

The Cavendish family is also tied up with another dukedom, that of Portland. In 1606 Sir Charles Cavendish, brother of the 1st Earl of Devonshire and third son of Bess Hardwick, settled on the estate of Welbeck Abbey in Nottinghamshire. The Abbey was later confiscated in the Civil War by parliament; but it was eventually bought back by the Cavendishs from whom it descended in the eighteenth century to Lady Margaret Harley. 'My noble, lovely little Peggy' (as Prior described her) was the considerable heiress of the 2nd Earl of Oxford and his Cavendish bride. Peggy married the 2nd Duke of Portland and the thoroughfares of Marylebone in London still bear eloquent witness to this union—Harley Street, Welbeck Street, Portland Place, Cavendish Square, and so on.

The 2nd Duke of Portland, chiefly notable for his good looks, was the grandson of William III's friend and compatriot, Hans William Bentinck. As a boy Bentinck had endeared himself to the young Prince of Orange by absorbing some of William's smallpox fever through sleeping beside him for sixteen days and nights. Unfortunately the British did not take kindly to this Dutch favourite who became the 1st Earl of Portland. The Duke of Marlborough found him 'a wooden fellow', while Swift considered him 'as great a Dunce as ever I knew'.

The 3rd Duke of Portland hardly won golden opinions either in his two brief spells as Prime Minister. He married his cousin, Lady Dorothy Cavendish, daughter of the 4th Duke of Devonshire, and both took the surname of Cavendish-Bentinck. Their London home was Burlington House (now the Royal Academy) and their descendants include the Queen Mother, whose own mother Cecilia (or 'Celia')—a clergyman's daughter and a first cousin of the 6th Duke of Portland—was a Cavendish-Bentinck.

The 4th Duke of Portland (nicknamed 'Old Leather Breeches') was prompted by his third son, Lord George Bentinck, to buy the Hughenden estate in Buckinghamshire for Disraeli in 1847. Lord George was himself a colourful politician and a noted figure on the Turf; like his two brothers he remained a bachelor. The second brother became the notoriously eccentric 5th Duke. A man of solitary disposition—rather like his cousin, the mad scientist Henry Cavendish—the 5th Duke of Portland had been spurned in love by the Covent Garden singer Adelaide Kemble. He adopted a highly individual sartorial manner: his trousers would be secured above the ankle by a piece of string, a vast coat and umbrella were employed to protect his privacy and on top of his long brown wig he perched to a two foot high hat. Despite this bizarre get-up, no one was allowed to notice him; the instructions at Welbeck were to pass him by 'as they would a tree'.

Although the 5th Duke of Portland made the Abbey into a splendid palace he did not go in for entertaining. He preferred to confine himself to limited quarters, with a letterbox in his bedroom door as a means of communication, lunching off one half of a fowl, and dining off the other. Above—or rather below—all, he is best remembered for the extraordinary subterranean building operations at Welbeck. These included the astonishing ballroom—said to be the largest room in Europe without supporting pillars—and the miles of tunnels. The riding school he built is second only in size to the Spanish Riding School in Vienna.

For all his eccentricity, the 5th Duke of Portland was a generous landlord and a pubic-spirited philanthropist. His reclusive habits, however, enabled an Australian claimant to cobble together a famous lawsuit based on the fallacy that the Duke had led a 'double life' as a Baker Street shopkeeper. As the judge observed, the case merely afforded 'one more striking proof of the unfathomable depths of human credulity'.

The 6th Duke of Portland, a halfbrother of the Bohemian hostess Lady Ottoline Morrell, succeeded his strange cousin in 1879 and took advantage of his predecessor's building work, entertaining lavishly at Welbeck. One of his guests, though, Archduke Franz Ferdinand of Austria, was nearly shot by a loader on a shoot just a year before Sarajevo. A champion of the Turf, like Lord George Bentinck, the 6th Duke put his earnings from racing to good use, building old people's homes known as 'The Winnings'. His Duchess, Winifred, was also much more than the beautiful Edwardian hostess portrayed by Sargent, taking a special interest in the welfare of the miners on this private domain in the 'Dukeries'. Before the 6th Duke died, the Portlands moved to a smaller modern house on the estate and the Abbey later became a military college, though the staterooms are still splendidly maintained by a venerable female retainer.

The 16,000 acre estate is now owned by Lady Anne Bentinck, daughter of the 7th Duke of Portland (known as 'Chopper' from his days in the carpentry workshop at Eton), upon whose death in 1977 the Dukedom passed to a junior line. It now seems destined for extinction, though the Earldom of Portland will continue through the Counts Bentinck.

Among their many peerage creations the Stuarts also ennobled the descendants of some of the Tudor 'new men'. Families representing such creations today include the Montagus, Fanes, Grevilles and Thynnes; and the Duke of Marlborough, Earl Spencer and Viscount Churchill all descend in the male line from Sir Robert Spencer, a powerful figure under Queen Elizabeth who was made Baron Spencer by James I.

The fortunes of the Spencer dynasty at the beginning of the Tudor period were founded on sheep. 'My lord, when these things were doing your ancestors were keeping sheep', said the 'Collecting Earl' of Arundel to the 1st Lord Spencer during a parliamentary debate about the royal prerogative in 1621.

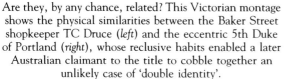

Are they, by any chance, related? This Victorian montage shows the physical similarities between the Baker Street shopkeeper TC Druce (*left*) and the eccentric 5th Duke of Portland (*right*), whose reclusive habits enabled a later Australian claimant to the title to cobble together an unlikely case of 'double identity'.

Lord George Bentinck, the early nineteenth-century politician and racing man.

Lord Spencer had this reply for his proud Howard adversary: 'When my ancestors were keeping sheep, Your Lordship's ancestors were plotting treason'.

The 1st Lord Spencer was reputed to have more ready money than anyone else in the kingdom thanks to his 19,000 sheep and to his shrewd dealings in cattle, rye and barley. The 2nd Lord Spencer's wife was the daughter of Shakespeare's patron, the Earl of Southampton, and their eldest son, Henry, married the lady immortalized as 'Sacharissa' by the poet Edmund Waller. Henry lent Charles I £20,000 at the beginning of the Civil War and was created Earl of Sunderland, only to be killed four months later at the Battle of Newbury.

This gallant Spencer Cavalier's son, the brilliant and much feared 2nd Earl of Sunderland, was the wily lieutenant of Charles II, James II and, even, of William III. His remarkable career included stints as ambassador to Paris, Cologne and Madrid and the *Dictionary of National Biography* sums him up as 'the craftiest, most rapacious and most unscrupulous of all the politicians of the second half of the 17th century'.

The diarist John Evelyn described the rooms and furnishings at the Spencer seat of Althorp, which the 2nd Earl of Sunderland Italianized, as 'such as may become a great prince'. Althorp, originally a redbrick moated courtyard house, was later remodelled by the fashionable Whig architect Henry Holland.

In 1699 the 3rd Earl of Sunderland, who was to become one of the Principal Secretaries in the reigns of Queen Anne and of George I, before burning his fingers over the 'South Sea Bubble', married the daughter of the great military genius, the Duke of Marlborough. This marrige marked the beginning of the divide in the Spencer family for, after the death of their elder son, the 4th Earl of Sunderland, the next son, Charles succeeded to the Earldom of Sunderland and then to the Dukedom of Marlborough. As the great Duke's only son died of smallpox as a boy, the Dukedom had passed under the special remainder to his elder daughter. Her son predeceased her so the Dukedom and the Blenheim estates passed to her eldest surviving nephew, Charles Spencer, 5th Earl of Sunderland.

The new Duke of Marlborough's younger brother, John Spencer, succeeded to Althorp and was the ancestor of the present line of Earls Spencer. Thus it is that the present Duke of Marlborough, who bears the surname of Spencer-Churchill, is in fact the senior descendant in the male line of the 1st Lord Spencer.

It is an enjoyable twist of history that there was an earlier Lady Diana Spencer who was lined up as a possible bride for an earlier Prince of Wales. This Lady Diana was the sister of Charles, Duke of Marlborough and John Spencer, the two progenitors of the separate branches of the family. 'The person, the merit and the family of Lady Diana Spencer', wrote an unsuccessful claimant to her hand, the 4th Earl of Chesterfield, to the Lady's grandmother, Sarah, Duchess of Marlborough, 'are objects so valuable that they must necessarily have . . . caused many applications of this nature to Your Grace'.

The formidable Sarah (once described as 'that BBBB old B' by her creditor Sir John Vanbrugh, the architect of Blenheim) plotted a secret marriage between Lady Diana and George II's unsatisfactory son, Frederick Louis. This was the Prince of Wales known to history as 'Poor Fred, who was alive and is now dead'. A dowry of £100,000 was baited for the bankrupt Prince, but Sarah's scheme came to naught after Sir Robert Walpole, the first 'Prime Minister', got wind of it.

Sarah, Duchess of Marlborough, had a soft spot for her grandson John Spencer, the squire of Althorp, to whom she left a considerable fortune and the Marlborough plate. This branch of the Spencers has been noted for its connoisseurship and skill in accumulating and arranging a remarkably fine collection of works of art. The 1st Earl Spencer, who built Spencer House overlooking London's Green Park, was a friend of Sir Joshua Reynolds, who painted his Countess and their daughter Georgiana, Duchess of Devonshire.

The 2nd Earl Spencer, a prominent Whig, was First Lord of the Admiralty at the time of Trafalgar; and the 3rd Earl was also a successful politician, becoming Chancellor of the Exchequer and promoting the Reform Bill; but his main love was farming. The next Earl was an Admiral and took an old salt's view of discipline: when his daughter was disobedient, he did not hesitate to lock her up in a cupboard under the stairs.

Admiral Earl Spencer's son was known as the 'Red Earl' on account of his long red beard, and the Seymour girl he married came to be known as 'Spencer's Fairy Queen'. The Red Earl had two spells as Lord Lieutenant of Ireland, but was happiest in the hunting field. He often rode out with the beautiful Empress Elisabeth of Austria, a frequent guest at Althorp. The Red Earl's halfbrother succeeded as the 6th Earl Spencer and also became the third member of the family to become Lord Chamberlain.

The present Princess of Wales's close connections with the Court can, indeed, hardly be overstated. Her paternal grandmother was a member of the Queen Mother's household—as her maternal grandmother, Ruth Lady Fermoy still is—and the princess's father, the present Earl Spencer, is a former equerry to the Queen. On the morning of his youngest daughter's wedding day in 1981, Lord Spencer, whose determination to play his part despite his frail health was one of the features of that wonderful occasion, said that in vowing to help her country for the rest of her life Lady Diana would be 'following in the tradition of her ancestors'.

Perhaps the greatest of all the Princess of Wales's ancestors, John Churchill, 1st Duke of Marlborough, was the son of a commoner and started life without the prospect of inheriting either a title or large estates. He is one of the very few examples in British history of a successful man from comparatively obscure beginnings who has rocketed to dukedom. For all his brilliant achievements, though, it should be remembered that he owed his early advancement to the fact that his sister, Arabella Churchill, was the mistress of the Duke of York, the future James II.

From the time the triumphant soldier's grandson, the 5th Earl of Sunderland, succeeded to the Dukedom of Marlborough up until 1817 the dukes bore the surname of Spencer alone. Then the bibliophile 5th Duke of Marlborough assumed the additional surname of Churchill to commemorate the victor of Blenheim. Before he succeeded to the Dukedom, the 5th Duke was styled, by courtesy, Marquess of Blandford and it is noteworthy that he was the first nobleman to spell 'Marquess' thus instead of the previously traditional 'Marquis'. The latter spelling is still used in Scotland on account of the 'Auld Alliance' with France.

Subsequent Dukes of Marlborough lived, almost inevitably, in the shadow of the great Duke and few made much of an impact on public life. The 7th Duke was the Lord Lieutenant of Ireland and his wife was inordinately proud of a letter she once received from Queen Victoria praising her fund-raising activities. 'You realize', the Duchess used to tell her grandson while brandishing this royal epistle, 'that in my life, I have been of some use to my fellow subjects'.

The late-Victorian 8th Duke of Marlborough was no mean scientist; indeed it has been said that he anticipated some of Edison's inventions. Unfortunately, however, he robbed Blenheim of the great Duke's incomparable collection of pictures by selling them at Christie's in 1886 and spent the proceeds on converting some of the bedrooms of Vanbrugh's monumental Palace into laboratories for his electrical experiments and also on putting up orchid houses. Someone who spent a night in one of the converted bedrooms shortly after the 8th Duke's premature death in 1892 claimed to have had a disagreeable psychical experience—similar to sleeping with a corpse that was emitting electric shocks.

Scabrous stories were told about the 'wicked' 8th Duke of Marlborough's immorality and he gained notoriety through his divorce. His wife, an Abercorn Hamilton, who was much given to practical jokes in the worst taste (such as placing a celluloid baby on her husband's breakfast tray instead of a poached egg), cited the Countess of Aylesford in the case shortly before her husband succeeded to the Dukedom. Lady Aylesford had already borne him a son, when she made a sensational elopement with Lord Blandford, the future 8th Duke, the repercussions of which involved Albert Edward, Prince of Wales. After the Prince had called Blandford a blackguard, the latter's brother, Lord Randolph Churchill, took the astonishing step of trying to blackmail the heir to the throne using some compromising letters that the Prince himself had written to Lady Aylesford.

'The Shooting Party' by John Wootton, showing John Spencer MP
(the father of the 1st Earl Spencer), Ranger of Windsor Great Park,
enjoying a day's sport with the 3rd Duke of Queensberry.

The melancholy features of the meteoric politician Lord Randolph Churchill who resigned too hastily and died of syphilis.

Winston Churchill (in bow tie) and other members of a house party at Blenheim Palace watching the Yeomanry Sports.

The great Derbyshire heiress 'Bess of Hardwick' (died 1607),
who, as Lodge tells us, 'unsated with the wealth and caresses
of three husbands, she finished her conquests by marrying the
Earl of Shrewsbury, the richest and most powerful peer of his
time', and after his death she built the H-shaped Hardwick Hall
where this portrait now hangs.

The south and east fronts of Plas Newydd, beside the Menai Strait, seat of the Pagets, Marquesses of Anglesey. Now owned by the National Trust, the house is best known for its enchanting *trompe l'œil* murals by Rex Whistler.

The Marchioness of Tavistock, bloodstock breeder and chatelaine of Woburn Abbey, the showplace of the Russell family in Bedfordshire where the numerous facilities include a golf course (see the bunkers in the background).

Sir Joshua Reynolds's tender portrait of Georgiana, wife
of the 1st Earl Spencer, with her daughter and namesake,
the famous 'face without a frown' who was to marry, in 1774,
the 5th Duke of Devonshire.

The 6th Duke of Devonshire out shooting with Mr Beaumont, as portrayed by RR Reinagle (at Chatsworth). The 'Bachelor Duke', as he was known, was described by his contemporary, the 9th Duke of Argyll, as 'the model of the old English noble of his time'.

Like his brother, the 8th Duke of Marlborough, Lord Randolph Churchill was a strange and unhappy character. After a meteoric political career in which he rose to being Chancellor of the Exchequer in his thirties, the erratic Lord Randolph resigned too hastily and eventually died of syphilis. It is sometimes said that there is 'bad blood' somewhere in the Spencer-Churchills.

Notwithstanding the family failings, to have produced a second national hero in Britain's Second World War saviour, Winston Churchill, is certainly something to be reckoned with. Sir Winston, Lord Randolph's elder son, born at Blenheim, was at one stage the heir presumptive to the Dukedom. He was later offered a dukedom of his own by the present Queen, but he declined the honour, preferring to stay in the House of Commons.

Winston's mother, the spirited American, Jennie Jerome, was one of several Spencer-Churchill brides to come from the United States of America. His cousin, the 9th Duke of Marlborough—whose sobriquet of 'Sunny' derived from his early courtesy style of Sunderland, rather than his far from cheerful disposition—accounted for a couple of them. First, there was that tragically unhappy heiress Consuelo Vanderbilt, dragooned into marrying a nobleman about whom she knew little and cared less, by her ambitious mother. 'Your first duty is to have a child', Consuelo was told by the haughty Dowager of the 7th Duke of Marlborough at their first meeting, 'and it must be a son because it would be intolerable to have that little upstart Winston become Duke. Are you in the family way?'

After the divorce from Consuelo, who produced two sons, the 9th Duke of Marlborough married the Grecian beauty, Gladys Deacon. Her Bostonian background and European adventures were reminiscent of a Henry James novel. Once the toast of *la belle époque*, Gladys became a recluse, before being dragged off to end her days as an almost-forgotten figure in a psycho-geriatric ward.

The present Duke of Marlborough's brother also married an American heiress first time around, whereas his own second wife was formerly married to Aristotle Onassis, the Greek shipowner. Their late father, Bert, the 10th Duke of Marlborough, is the subject of numerous tales that belong to aristocratic folklore, such as his inquiry—when away from Blenheim—as to why his toothbrush was not foaming properly. The reason turned out to be that no toothpaste had been applied, a service usually performed, unbeknown to the Duke, by his absent valet.

Beyond the peerage—and for that matter, the baronetage—an outstanding example of a 'great commoner' family that was founded by a prominent seventeenth-century figure is the Bankes family of Kingston Lacy. Sir John Bankes, Chief Justice of the Common Pleas in the reign of Charles I, bought extensive lands in Dorset and also the old royal fortress of Corfe Castle which he made his home. Corfe was blown up on Cromwell's orders after the Chief Justice's wife had valiantly defended it on behalf of the

King in two memorable sieges. Lady Bankes was ultimately betrayed by an officer of the garrison and this treachery led to the fall of the Castle. As a mark of respect for this plucky woman, the full honours of war were accorded on her departure.

Corfe was replaced as the family seat by the splendid Carolean mansion of Kingston Lacy, built by Sir Ralph Bankes in 1663 and embellished and filled with art treasures by subsequent generations of the family, notably William John Bankes, whose wanderings took him as far afield as the Euphrates. In 1833 Bankes stood trial for homosexual importuning but, thanks to the evidence of the Duke of Wellington, the Headmaster of Harrow and various other highly respected friends, he was acquitted. Eight years later, however, he was charged with a similar offence. This time he jumped bail and left to spend the rest of his life in exile in Venice.

He was succeeded at Kingston Lacy by his brother George, a politician who became Secretary of the Board of Control and a Privy Councillor; one of his younger sons won a posthumous VC at Lucknow during the Indian Mutiny. The late Ralph Bankes, George's great-grandson, was called to the Bar, but devoted his life to the 16,000 acre Dorset estate—now a gloriously rural oasis in this increasingly overcrowded corner of the south-west coast. The squire died in 1981, leaving the property—including Corfe Castle, Badbury Rings, the 'Old Harry' rock and Kingston Lacy—to the National Trust.

It is indeed hard to think of a better example of a 'great commoner' family than the Bankeses of Kingston Lacy: they were neither recusants nor a branch of a titled family, none of them has ever held an hereditary honour; Henry Bankes, father of the errant connoisseur and of the politician, was offered a peerage but refused it, saying that he preferred to be plain Mr Bankes of Kingston Lacy.

CHAPTER V

WHIG MAGNATES

THE EIGHTEENTH CENTURY

I N THE EIGHTEENTH CENTURY, that age of Whig supremacy, Crown favour was no longer a means of social advancement as it had been under the Tudors and Stuarts. The great landowning families were largely able to close their ranks against outsiders. The aristocracy was then at its richest, most independent and most powerful, coming the nearest in its history to a closed corporation.

The Whig party had helped put the House of Hanover on the British throne and, as parliament grew more powerful at the expense of the Crown, the grandeur of the Whig magnates began to know no bounds. Their magnificent London houses, such as Devonshire House and Shelburne House, took the place of the Court as the centre of aristocratic life. On their broad acres arose splendid Palladian country houses, like Holkham and Stowe, filled with works of art from Italy and set in romantic landscapes created by William Kent and Capability Brown.

The parliamentary boroughs were controlled by the magnates who nominated their members to sit in the House of Commons. The electoral system was certainly corrupt, with its 'rotten' and 'pocket' boroughs: for instance, the constituency of Old Sarum consisted of a heap of stones and seven voters under the sway of the Pitt family. Nevertheless, it can be argued that the quality of intellect and ability in the Commons was probably higher than at any other period of British history.

The great Whig magnates were, broadly speaking, the descendants of the rich landowners of Tudor and Stuart England grown richer still. It was easy in the eighteenth century for existing peers to use their parliamentary 'interest' to be promoted up the ranks of the peerage, and for the heirs of extinct peerages to obtain new creations. But for commoners to enter the peerage was more difficult, at any rate until the number of creations increased with the administration of the Younger Pitt.

The majority of the families who first rose to the peerage in the eighteenth century were of solid county stock, often of medieval knightly origin, who had owned estates for several centuries. Examples of 'great commoner' dynasties of this sort would include: the Herveys; the Wodehouses (whose cadets included the immortal PG); the Lowthers (the family of the Edwardian 'Yellow' Earl of Lonsdale who spent £3,000 a year on cigars alone); the Fortescues; the Curzons; the Grimstons; and the de Greys (a lavatory at whose seat in Norfolk contains the 6th Lord Walsingham's shooting record of 1,070 grouse in fourteen hours eighteen minutes). Two of these long-established great commoner families, the Grosvenors and the Gowers, eventually rose to dukedoms in the following century.

The Grosvenors obtained fabulous riches by the marriage in 1677 of Sir Thomas Grosvenor to Mary Davis, heiress of her father's London property which included most of present-day Mayfair and Belgravia. A century later, Sir Richard Grosvenor became Earl Grosvenor; his son rose to being Marquess of Westminster and, in 1874, the 3rd Marquess became a Duke. The Dukedom of Westminster is effectively the last entirely non-royal ducal creation. It was conferred on a distinguished public figure who happened to be a marquess; whereas his grandfather, also a distinguished public figure, was made a marquess having formerly been a very rich earl. Thus, like the great majority of British ducal families, the Grosvenors, rose to their Dukedom by moving gradually up the scale of the peerage.

The vast wealth of the 1st Duke of Westminster was of vital significance in his elevation to a dukedom. The old theory about the 'endowment' of peerages, whereby they were expected to be supported by an appropriately sized landed estate, still very much applied. There have been peers at various times in the past who refused dukedoms on the grounds that they were not rich enough to support the dignity. A case in point is the 5th Marquess of Lansdowne, Foreign Secretary at the end of the nineteenth century, whose Marquessate was originally created for his ancestor, the 2nd Earl of Shelburne, Prime Minister in the early 1780s. Once described by an American ambassador as the most complete aristocrat he had ever met, the 5th Lord Lansdowne was offered and declined a Dukedom on his return from being Viceroy of India. The present Marquess of Lansdowne pursued the political tradition of his family, holding government office in Harold Macmillan's administrations.

Perhaps because of their late-nineteenth-century Dukedom, some people seem to labour under the delusion that the Grosvenors are rather on the *nouveau* side. Nothing could be further from the truth. In fact they are a very long-established Cheshire family traceable to at least the twelfth century. The Grosvenors came into the Eaton estate in Cheshire through marriage to the heiress of that property in the reign of Henry VI. The first house on the present site was built from 1675 onwards by Sir Thomas Grosvenor, husband of the great London heiress Mary Davis. Sir Thomas's great-grandfather had been made a Baronet by James I. Eaton was subsequently enlarged for the 1st Marquess of Westminster and then, for the 1st Duke, totally transformed into an overwhelming Gothic palace by Alfred Waterhouse, at a cost of over £½ million.

The 1st Duke of Westminster was a liberal and enlightened landlord who did much to improve that part of London in which his estates were situated. Belgravia, incidentally and oddly, takes its name from a tiny hamlet of three cottages on the Eaton estate. A philanthropist and public figure, the Duke collected pictures and was a patron of the Turf, winning the Derby four times. His first winner was called 'Bend Or' in commemoration of the coat of arms used by medieval Grosvenors. This famous coat, which contains one of the simplest shields in English heraldry (*azure, a bend or*, ie a gold stripe against a blue background) was the subject of the first recorded armorial trial in the Court of Chivalry in 1385, when the 1st Lord Scrope of Bolton successfully challenged Sir Robert le Grosvenor's right to bear the coat of arms.

The 1st Duke of Westminster's horse was, in turn, the source of the sobriquet of the 2nd Duke, who was a much more controversial character. A brave soldier reputed to have narrowly missed a VC in the First World War, an all-round sportsman, an excellent and generous landlord, Bend Or was also an undeniably selfish, spoilt, thrice-divorced playboy. James Lees-Milne once described the third Duchess's married life as 'a definition of unadulterated hell'. Bend Or's fourth and final wife, Anne (or 'Nancy'), became famous in widowhood as the owner of that legendary Irish steeplechaser, Arkle.

The story goes that it was the 2nd Duke of Westminster who hounded his more publicly distinguished brother-in-law, Earl Beauchamp, out of society and into exile on account of that unfortunate figure's alleged behaviour with footmen. It is possible that Evelyn Waugh may have had the Earl in mind when creating the character of Lord Marchmain in *Brideshead Revisited*, as Waugh was a friend of the Lygon family and used to stay at their seat of Madresfield Court in Worcestershire.

Bend Or's lasting claim to fame may well be the celebrated exchange in Noel Coward's *Private Lives*. (Scene: a balcony on the Riviera. Amanda — 'Whose yacht is that?' Elyot — 'The Duke of Westminster's I expect. It always is'.) In fact he had two yachts, a steam yacht and a sailing ship. While living extravagantly, the 2nd Duke of Westminster was also a shrewd businessman. He increased the family fortunes by buying property in many different countries, thus skilfully spreading the resources of the immensely wealthy Grosvenor estate. He sold Grosvenor House (noted for its fine gates, ballroom and garden) in the 1920s for about £½ million, and it was promptly pulled down — to be replaced by an hotel and a block of flats.

Eaton Hall itself was given up by the 2nd Duke on the outbreak of the Second World War and was subsequently leased to the War Office as an Officers' Cadet School. At the end of National Service in the early 1960s, however, the family decided that this Victorian extravaganza was in too poor a condition, and too large, to restore. Thus, sadly, it was demolished.

None the less, Waterhouse's chapel and the 'Big Ben'-like clocktower have been retained to form a dramatic contrast to the house recently built at Eaton by the present young Duke of Westminster. Whatever one thinks of its modernist architecture, the scale of this remarkable new ducal seat has certainly not been equalled by any other country house of the modern age. Its principal rooms form a *piano nobile* on the first floor above, among other features, a swimming-pool, and a games room.

The young old-Harrovian Duke is married to a granddaughter of the late Lady Zia Wernher, originally a member of the Russian imperial family. The Duchess's sister is married to the Duke of Abercorn, a magnate in Northern Ireland, where the late Duke of Westminster ('Pud') also spent most of his time. The present Duke's second sister is married to another young Duke, Roxburghe, holder of the last Scottish peerage to be created before the Act of Union in 1707. The elder Grosvenor sister, Leonora, was formerly married to the Earl of Lichfield, the ubiquitous photographer who heads another family that first entered the peerage in the eighteenth century, in the person of Admiral Lord Anson.

The rise of the Grosvenors is somewhat comparable to that of another powerful ducal dynasty, the Leveson Gowers, Dukes of Sutherland. The Gowers were a long-established Yorkshire family of Baronets who became rich in the seventeenth century through marriage with the coal-mining Midland heiress, Frances Leveson. Sir John Leveson Gower became the 1st Lord Gower in 1703, his son became an Earl, his grandson Marquess of Stafford; and the 2nd Marquess, who married the Scottish Countess of Sutherland in her own right, was made Duke of Sutherland by William IV.

In the early eighteenth century, the Gowers were Tories, a party that suffered from the stigma of Jacobitism, but they changed sides and during the Jacobite '45 rebellion even raised a regiment of sorts against Bonnie Prince Charlie. Dr Johnson took a dim view of this ratting and when explaining the word 'renegado' for his great *Dictionary* wrote: 'one who deserts to the enemy, a revolter, sometimes we say a Gower'. (As so often happens, a third party removed this crack before printing.)

Both the 1st Earl Gower and the 1st Marquess of Stafford were Lords Privy Seal and the latter refused the Prime Ministership in 1783, though subsequently served in Pitt's first administration as Lord President of the Council. He had also held this post in the unhappy government of Lord North, who lost the American colonies, but resigned in recriminatory heat in 1799, saying that 'no man of honour or conscience could any longer sit there'.

The 1st Marquess of Stafford married the heiress Lady Louisa Egerton, niece of that founder of inland navigation, the 3rd Duke of Bridgwater. The celebrated Bridgwater canals brought yet more enormous revenues into the Leveson Gower family.

The vast Gothic palace of Eaton Hall, Cheshire, built by
Alfred Waterhouse for the 1st Duke of Westminster.
Constructed between 1870 and 1883, it was demolished in the
1960s and replaced by a new house in the Modern style.

The present Duke of Westminster, landlord of Mayfair and
Belgravia.

The 2nd Marquess of Stafford, described by Greville as a 'leviathan of wealth', achieved the grandest match—at least on paper—by snapping up the 'Great Lady of the Clan Sutherland'. However, the Sutherland acreage in Scotland, incredibly vast as it was, did not actually signify as much as the Leveson estates in Staffordshire. The great wealth came not from these barren tracts of the poor and remote Scottish county from which the Leveson Gowers took their Dukedom, but from the coal on their relatively modest 12,000 acres in the Midlands.

After her husband received his Dukedom, the 'Great Lady of Sutherland' became known as the 'Duchess-Countess'. She seems to have had rather more 'go' in her than the dull Duke—being noted for beauty, what Byron called princessly manners, painting water-colours and her correspondence with Sir Walter Scott. At one stage her husband was advised to forgo sexual relations, apparently in the hope of improving his eyesight. Unfortunately, during this sentence of celibacy, the spirited Elizabeth became pregnant, the father being popularly identified as her husband's brother-in-law, the 5th Earl of Carlisle.

The son from this supposed liaison, Lord Francis Leveson Gower, was certainly very unlike his putative father; Creevey defied anyone to receive 'greater civility' that he had done from this learned and cultivated patrician and Greville observed that Lord Francis 'regarded with indifference the ordinary objects of worldly ambition'. The latter diarist (who was Lord Francis's brother-in-law) said that 'He lived in and for his family, and he was their joy, their delight and their pride'.

On his 'official' father's death in 1883, Lord Francis Leveson Gower inherited the Egerton estates (including the great family collection of pictures) and took that surname, becoming Earl of Ellesmere thirteen years later. His descendant inherited the Dukedom of Sutherland in 1963 when the senior male line of the Leveson Gowers died out. The Earldom of Sutherland then passed to the late Duke's niece Elizabeth, who is married to the journalist Charles Janson.

Lord Francis Leveson Gower's almost-deaf elder brother, the 2nd Duke of Sutherland, who had suffered in his younger days from the pangs of unrequited love for the strong-minded Queen Louise of Prussia, was again somewhat overshadowed by his wife, Duchess Harriet, a close friend and Mistress of the Robes to Queen Victoria. 'I have come from my house to your palace', said the Queen to the Duchess on one of her frequent visits to Stafford House, the Sutherlands' imposing metropolitan mansion near St James's in London. Here in 1848, Chopin played before the Queen on one of the Sutherlands' musical evenings.

Duchess Harriet and her husband certainly lived on the grand scale. As well as enlarging and improving Stafford House (formerly York House and later renamed Lancaster House by Lever, the soap magnate) in London, they also rebuilt Lilleshall Hall in Shropshire, Trentham Hall in Staffordshire and

Stafford House, the London residence of the Dukes of
Sutherland, *en fête* for a reception in aid of the Lifeboat
Institution.

Cliveden in Buckinghamshire. For good measure they made extensive altera-tions to the Sutherland stronghold, Dunrobin Castle.

Duchess Harriet was a granddaughter of Georgiana, Duchess of Devon-shire. Her aunt, Harriet Cavendish, had also married into the Leveson Gowers in the shape of a younger brother of the 1st Duke of Sutherland. This Lord Granville Leveson Gower, a minor Canningite politician whose ambassadorial achievements were somewhat handicapped by the illegibility of his despatches, became 1st Earl Granville. Plain and practical, Aunt Harriet coped admirably with the problems caused by the fact that her husband, a gambler with winning blue eyes, had previously been the lover of her own aunt, the Countess of Bessborough — the problems taking the shape of a couple of bastard daughters. Harriet Countess of Granville's correspon-dence was noted for its witty observation of aristocratic life, though she succumbed to religiosity in her widowhood.

Lord Granville was fortunate to escape being murdered in the House of Commons in 1812. A deranged timber merchant with a grievance against Granville shot the Prime Minister, poor old Spencer Perceval, by mistake. Later, however, Lord Granville was peppered in Suffolk by the Iron Duke of Wellington, a notoriously bad shot, who also bagged a brace of dogs on the same outing. The present Earl Granville's mother was a sister of Queen Elizabeth the Queen Mother.

The main branch of the Leveson Gower family is, of course, notorious for its part in the early nineteenth-century 'Highland Clearances'. In a shameful episode of Scottish history, landowners forced the smaller Highland tenants off their land, in order to make larger and more up-to-date holdings. But it is worth remembering that — as is so often the case — their methods, though they caused terrible sufferings, were inspired by progressive economic theories and reforming zeal. The Edinburgh economists of the day had much to answer for.

The agricultural 'improvements' of the Victorian 3rd Duke of Sutherland, a liberal of advanced views, were of a more sympathetic nature. He enter-tained Garibaldi on his visit to London in 1864, as well as lending the Italian freedom fighter his yacht for use in the 'Risorgimento'. His youngest brother was the aesthetic homosexual, Lord Ronald Gower, a prolific author and Oscar Wilde's supposed model for Lord Henry Wootton in The Picture of Dorian Gray.

The 4th Duke of Sutherland was a fairly uninspiring figure with yet another remarkable wife, 'Meddlesome Millie', whose do-goodery in the Potteries was satirized by Arnold Bennett. In her Edwardian heyday this Duchess was a much admired beauty and hostess, but she also — if not quite to the extent of her halfsister, Daisy, Countess of Warwick — professed socialism and wrote some sentimental books. While Millie wanted to 'float on a lotus leaf on the waters of fancy', the Duke was more concerned about the effluent from the Potteries flowing through his grounds at Trentham. When the county council suggested (after he had offered it for educational purposes) that the palace should be used as a training college for women teachers, the Duke objected strongly and later razed it to the ground. In his younger days, the 4th Duke had had his stepmother sent to prison for destroying one of his father's documents.

The present Countess of Sutherland, a niece of the 5th Duke, still owns Dunrobin Castle, which has been used as a school in recent years. The heir to the Sutherland estates is her son, Lord Strathnaver, who married an American and served for five years with the Metropolitan Police.

Whereas the Grosvenors, Gowers and other 'great commoners' mentioned earlier in this chapter were of medieval descent, others were of newer family, though very much established by the time they were ennobled in the eighteenth century. Prominent among the families of Tudor foundation who entered the peerage in this period are the Cokes, owners of that quintessential Whig palace, Holkham Hall in Norfolk.

The Cokes descend from the eminent lawyer of the time of James I, Sir Edward Coke. Various claims have been made as to their origins. According to Walter Rye's *Songs, Stories, and Sayings of Norfolk*, the family 'really owe their surname to some excellent ancient caterer whose merits earned him the distinction of *the* Cook "le Cok"'.

The great family seat of Holkham, the apotheosis of the English Palladian movement with its stupendous marble hall, was begun in 1734 by Thomas Coke, Lord Lovel, an enthusiastic member of Lord Burlington's architectural group. The work was finished a few years after Thomas's death in 1759 by which time he had risen to the Earldom of Leicester. A friend and neighbour of Sir Robert Walpole at Houghton, this Lord Leicester was described by Sir Charles Hanbury-Williams as the oddest character in town—'a lover, statesman, connoisseur, buffoon'.

As well as filling Holkham with a magnificent collection of works of art, Lord Leicester was also an ardent supporter of cock-fighting. His death seems to have occurred as the result of a duel with another Norfolk neighbour, the future 1st Marquess Townshend. Lord Leicester's widow stayed on at Holkham, telling the eventual heir to the estate to 'understand that I will live as long as I can'.

This heir was none other than the celebrated 'Coke of Norfolk', Thomas Coke, the greatest commoner of them all. His father, Wenman Roberts, was a nephew of Lord Leicester who took the name and arms of Coke. Though young Thomas could have had a peerage for the asking—it was usual at this time for an important title which had become extinct to be revived for whoever inherited the family estates—he consistently refused any honour.

'If he was to knight me', said Coke hearing of a plan afoot by the Prince Regent to award him the accolade, 'by God, I'll break his sword'. He apparently turned down five offers of peerages before eventually deciding to accept Earl Grey's invitation in 1831. Ironically, this proposal was promptly squashed by William IV on account of a disobliging reference made by Coke about George III ('the worst man that ever sat on a throne, that bloody King'). Then, at last, in 1837, the genial Lord Melbourne persuaded the young Queen Victoria to create Coke of Norfolk Earl of Leicester.

A robust Whig and Foxite, Coke of Norfolk was first and foremost an agriculturalist, perhaps doing more for farming than, in the words of *The Times*, 'any other human being'. He admitted to spending more than £½ million on the improvement of his vast landed estates, transforming unyielding acres to fertile soil which produced 'the finest corn this country can boast' (as the 1842 obituary in the *Gentleman's Magazine* recorded). However, this son of the soil had cut quite a dash in his youth, being known in Rome as 'the handsome Englishman'—and the portrait by Batoni at Holkham given him by his lover Princess Louise of Stolberg (Bonnie Prince Charlie's wife) bears this out. Happily Holkham has hardly been changed since it was built and today it is the seat of Viscount Coke, son and heir of the 6th Earl of Leicester (who lives in South Africa).

Most of the important eighteenth-century politicians came from substantial county families like the Grenvilles, Temples and Lytteltons. These formed a powerful cousinhood to which the Elder and Younger Pitt also belonged, as well as two other Prime Ministers, George Grenville and his son William. This great Whig cousinhood acquired numerous peerages during the eighteenth century: the Grenvilles, for instance, rose to the Marquessate of Buckingham and became Dukes of Buckingham and Chandos in 1822. Though the Dukedom and the Marquessate are now extinct, the cousinhood is still represented in the peerage, notably by Earl Temple of Stowe (now living in Australia) and by the two Lyttelton peers, Viscounts Cobham and Chandos.

The Lytteltons produced several eighteenth-century politicians, including the 1st Lord Lyttelton, whose biography was written by Dr Johnson, and the family has continued to be prominent in the nineteenth and twentieth centuries. One of the many sons of the Victorian Lord Lyttelton was private secretary to his uncle, Mr Gladstone. Another son, that popular figure Alfred Lyttelton, was Secretary of State for the Colonies, an office held in turn after the Second World War by Alfred's talented son, Oliver, who became the 1st Viscount Chandos of the present creation. Apart from his political achievements, the name of Oliver Lyttelton is commemorated on London's South Bank by one of the auditoria at the National Theatre which he did so much to bring into being.

The scholarly Victorian Lord Lyttelton's remarkable brood also included a general and a bishop who, like most of the family, was a legendary, not to say obsessive, cricketer. He once admitted that he could never walk up a

A contemporary impression of the cruel Highland Clearances
of the early nineteenth century — inspired by progressive
economic theories of 'land use' — on the estates of the
Dukes of Sutherland.

'Coke of Norfolk' inspects his sheep. The great Palladian
palace of Holkham can be seen in the background.

church aisle without bowling an imaginary off-break and wondering whether it would take spin. Many of the Lytteltons' cricketing triumphs, particularly those of Alfred, took place at Eton, though the late Lord Cobham, a former Governor-General of New Zealand and vice-captain of an MCC tour to the Antipodes, was never anywhere near a place in the Eton XI.

The family's connection with Eton, however, went considerably beyond the playing fields. Dr Edward Lyttelton (yet another of the prolific Lord Lyttelton's sons) was the school's Headmaster. His halfsister was the wife of a subsequent Headmaster, Dr Cyril Alington (whose daughter is also in the family's political tradition in being the wife of a former Prime Minister, Lord Home of the Hirsel); and his nephew was a housemaster. The latter, George Lyttelton, who is the father of 'Humph', the trumpeter, has won posthumous celebrity as the erudite and entertaining correspondent of his former pupil, Sir Rupert Hart-Davis. The author and critic Philip Ziegler has described their exchange of letters in the 1950s as an outstanding example of mid-twentieth-century civilization.

The present Lord Cobham still lives at the Worcestershire family seat of Hagley Hall, situated disturbingly near the suburban sprawl of Birmingham. There are also notable buildings in the park such as the Temple of Theseus and the picturesque 'ruined' mock castle (of which Horace Walpole sarcastically remarked that it had the 'true rust of the Barons' Wars'). Hagley itself came close to ruin in a fire in 1926, but it was well restored.

The rise in the eighteenth-century peerage of this great Whig cousinhood owed as much to broad acres as to political talent. It was indeed very difficult to obtain a peerage if one did not possess a large estate. The eighteenth-century political 'man of business', who was in parliament for many years and held office, seldom obtained the peerage that would have come to him as a matter of course in the nineteenth and twentieth centuries. Looking carefully at the eighteenth-century peerage creations, however, one is struck by how many were conferred upon successful lawyers and sailors.

While these legal and naval peerages can definitely be regarded as honours obtained by achievement rather than on account of family position, it does not mean that their first holders were necessarily self-made men. Thus Lord Chancellor Harcourt came of a family of the greatest antiquity; Admiral Earl Howe was himself the son of a peer. Nevertheless it is possible to find some men who, through their achievements on the Bench or the quarter-deck, rose from the middle classes to found aristocratic dynasties, such as John Scott, the son of a Newcastle merchant who ended up as Lord Chancellor and the Earl of Eldon.

Only seldom did money alone obtain entry into the eighteenth-century peerage. Perhaps five families owe their ennoblement to tycoons, namely that of Dundas, Marquesses of Zetland (who can be classified as Scottish); of Lascelles, Earls of Harewood; of Pleydell-Bouverie, Earls of Radnor; of Smith

A military review at Stowe House, Buckinghamshire, the
seat of the Dukes of Buckingham and Chandos which is now
a public school.

Sir Richard Sykes, 7th Baronet, of the talented and eccentric
family of Sledmere, on his travels in China in the 1930s.

(later Caringtons), Lords Carrington; and of Vanneck, Lord Huntingfield. But even so, the 1st Viscount Folkestone, ancestor of the Earls of Radnor, can be said to have been more of a county magnate than a tycoon, though his father Sir William Des Bouveries, was an eminent turkey merchant. Lords Carrington and Huntingfield both came from banking dynasties and the Lascelles fortune that built Harewood House in Yorkshire was founded on sugar and slaves in the West Indies.

Another great Yorkshire dynasty, the Sykeses of Sledmere, can be said to be one of the few families outside the peerage that rose to territorial magnate status in the eighteenth century. These wealthy Hull merchants — descended in turn from a long line of merchants in Leeds — inherited Sledmere from the Kirkbys in the middle of the eighteenth century. They then proceeded to reclaim a vast area of the Yorkshire Wolds.

What had previously been furze-break and rabbit-warren was transformed by the Sykeses into a magnificent agricultural estate of 34,000 acres which, in the nineteenth century, produced a rent of £35,000 a year. The agriculturalist, Reverend Mark Sykes, was created a Baronet in 1783 and the 2nd Baronet, Sir Christopher, greatly enlarged the house into a noble late-Georgian mansion. Capability Brown was employed to landscape the park, moving the village out of sight of the house itself. Unfortunately Sir Christopher's important collection of books in the superbly plastered great library at Sledmere was sold off by his son, Sir Tatton Sykes, because one of his favourite packs of hounds was in need of financial assistance.

This legendary sportsman ('Old Tat') was described as one of the three great sights of Yorkshire, along with York Minster and Fountains Abbey. Though he lived until 1863, Old Tat was a figure very much out of the eighteenth century. A stern father, he established a Spartan routine at Sledmere with regular recourse to the whip. He himself would rise at 5.30am and walk three or four miles up and down the length of the 120 foot library before breakfasting off a basin of new milk and an apple or gooseberry tart, garnished with lumps of mutton fat and occasionally supplemented by a glass of stout and cream.

Sir Tatton's son and namesake, the 5th Baronet, was even more eccentric: he was a flower-hating hypochondriac addicted to milk puddings. In 1911, towards the end of his reign at Sledmere, the house was gutted by fire. Sir Tatton was indulging in one of his favourite activities at the time: 'First . . . I must finish my pudding, finish my pudding', he said. He was later heard to observe: 'These things will happen, these things will happen.' Happily all was not lost and the house was excellently restored by a local architect. The Turkish Room at Sledmere dates from the fire, being built for the most distinguished member of the family, Sir Mark Sykes, 6th Baronet.

A man of delightful character and all-round brilliance, Sir Mark was a traveller in the Near East, an expert on the Ottoman Empire, a writer and a

The camera became an amusing adjunct of country-house
life at the end of the nineteenth century. Here is a family
group at Castle Combe Manor, Wiltshire, in the form of
a 'Jacob's Ladder'.

witty cartoonist. He was a Tory politician, strongly wedded to the aristocratic system, but also with an equally strong sense of aristocratic duty and a deep and practical concern for the underprivileged. During the First World War, he exercised a decisive influence on Britain's Near Eastern policy, and seemed destined to become one of his country's leaders, when, at the age of thirty-nine, he fell a victim to the devastating influenza epidemic of 1919.

His second son, Christopher, was the author of several distinguished books including a biography of Evelyn Waugh. Christopher Sykes's great-uncle and namesake, a minor politician, was the wretched butt of Albert Edward, Prince of Wales. Unfortunately the Prince discovered, when he poured a glass of brandy over his friend's head, that Christopher would try to maintain his dignity when the target of royal practical jokes—'As your Royal Highness pleases' was his only reaction. As another Christopher Sykes, a younger brother of the present Baronet, has related in his hilarious account of the family in *The Visitors Book*: poor old Christopher 'sacrificed his dignity, his fortune and finally his life to royalty'.

Sir Mark Sykes's youngest daughter, the artist Angela Countess of Antrim, also inherited her father's skills as a cartoonist, producing two jolly strips on the history of her own family and that of her husband. The present Baronet, another Sir Tatton Sykes, is a stylish bachelor who has recently been redecorating Sledmere, paying particular attention to the celebrated first-floor library.

The eighteenth century saw the growth of British commerce and overseas interests, so it was natural that a large number of new landed families should be founded, even if few could be said to have achieved the 'magnate' status of the Yorkshire Sykeses or the untitled brewing Whitbreads of Bedfordshire. The fact remained that the buying of a large landed estate was no easy matter in the era of the Whig magnates. Existing owners tended to be well off and unwilling to sell. The great families were in danger of becoming too much of a closed corporation.

CHAPTER VI

MERCHANT PRINCES

THE NINETEENTH AND
TWENTIETH CENTURIES

THE GREAT REFORM ACT of 1832 may have deprived the territorial magnates of their political power, but they continued to exert an important influence in nineteenth-century politics and, of course, went on growing richer. None the less, the Industrial Revolution produced its own 'new men', who were beginning to vie with the magnates in wealth. Britain's rapid economic growth and expansion overseas helped to put the aristocracy on a much broader base.

At the time of Waterloo, there were less than 500 people in England outside the landowning class with incomes in excess of £5,000 a year; by 1875 the number of business incomes exceeding £5,000 a year had multiplied by eight. Moreover, the great 'gentlemen' class of the nineteenth century embraced not only property and money but also the services and the professions. The proliferating public schools supplied the British Empire with a veritable 'service' aristocracy.

Land, though, remained the commodity that really counted and few of these service dynasties — some of which were certainly 'great' in their own way — were able to lay claim to broad acres. And for all their professed radicalism the new men of substance who came into political life in the nineteenth century were comfortably assimilated into the old order.

Of the early nineteenth-century peerage creations, the Dukedom of Wellington is outstanding, reflecting the increased importance of the army after the Napoleonic Wars. Unlike the great Duke of Marlborough, the 'Iron Duke' was not a self-made grandee, for the fact is that he was born with the prefix of 'Honourable', being the younger son of an Irish earl. Indeed he was close in the succession of the Wellesley family Earldom of Mornington which in the event passed to his son. As with the Dukes of Marlborough, the subsequent Dukes of Wellington have tended to live in the shadow of their famous forebear, though, unlike the Spencer-Churchill family, the Wellesleys have yet to produce a second national hero.

In the nineteenth century the business of politics began to count for more than mere status. Thus, although on the face of it the Earldom of Durham conferred upon the Lambtons of Lambton Castle (where they had been seated since medieval times) might seem in keeping with the old tradition of ennobling territorial dynasties, in fact the honour was very much earnt by the politician 'Radical Jack' Lambton, sometime Ambassador to Russia and Canadian Proconsul. The Earldom of Durham has now been disclaimed for life by his descendant Antony Lambton, the writer, whose own political career ended in the so-called 'sex scandal' of 1973 — an example of one of Britain's periodic wallows in prurient hypocrisy.

The pattern of the age saw the supremacy of the long-established county magnates being challenged by the newer families that had grown rich through commerce and industry. Although the magnates were richer than ever — the famous remark that one could 'jog along on seventy thousand a year' belongs to this period — the new men of the Industrial Revolution were beginning to vie with them in wealth. For instance, the Glamorgan iron-master, Sir Josiah Guest, bought an estate in Dorset and married an earl's daughter; their son, a steel tycoon, was created Lord Wimborne and married the daughter of a duke.

A later Lord Wimborne, who lived next door to the Ritz in London, was asked by the hotel how much he would like for his garden as they were thinking of extending their hotel. Lord Wimborne replied to the effect that he was thinking of extending his garden and wished to know how much they would take for the Ritz.

Several of the peerages given to nineteenth-century industrial dynasties were not so much on account of their industrial background, though, as owing to the fact one of their number was in the government. Politics was increasingly the means of social advancement. Thus Edward Strutt, a grandson of the Derby cotton spinner, Jedediah Strutt (partner of the great Sir Richard Arkwright), was made Lord Belper because he was a Privy Councillor and had served as Chancellor of the Duchy of Lancaster.

The Belper Strutts are not related to the Essex landowning family of that name which entered the peerage in 1821 with the Barony of Rayleigh, a title famous through the scientific achievements of the 3rd Baron, who discovered argon, and of his son, the 4th Baron. Many of their experiments were carried out at the family seat of Terling Place, if not always quite understood by the servants. The inventor of argon's gamekeeper once observed that 'his Lordship spends most of his time in his lavatory'.

The Smiths of WH Smith, the newsagents and stationers, became Viscounts Hambleden in the late nineteenth century but, again, this peerage owed more to politics than to papers. The original bookseller's son and namesake, William Henry Smith, was First Lord of the Treasury and Leader of the House of Commons under the Premiership of the 3rd Marquess of

THE MAKER OF MODERN EGYPT: LORD CROMER, HIS SUCCESSO

An *Illustrated London News* tribute to Evelyn Baring, a
scion of the banking family who became 'The Maker of
Modern Egypt' and, in 1901, the 1st Earl of Cromer.

Salisbury. Smith's surprising appointment to be First Lord of the Admiralty in 1877 inspired WS Gilbert to portray him as 'Sir Joseph Porter' (the 'Ruler of the Queen's Navee') in HMS *Pinafore*.

Chief among the families of the mercantile aristocracy which entered the peerage during the nineteenth century were the banking Barings. By 1900 there were four Baring peers (as a statistic it is of interest that there were actually seven peerages conferred in sixty-six years on members of the family) and today there are five. This impressive tally is due as much to the brilliance of many of the Barings as to their wealth. 'There are six great powers in Europe', said the Duc de Richelieu, '*viz.* England, France, Russia, Austria, Prussia and Baring Brothers'.

Originally a German family, the Barings settled in Devon in 1717. Johann Baring, the son of a Lutheran pastor in Bremen, was sent to Exeter in that year to be apprenticed to the Brothers Cock, a firm of manufacturers of a sort of cloth called 'Long Ells'. He married a well-to-do local girl who ran the family cloth business at Larkbeare nearby after his death. Later in the eighteenth century, Francis Baring, an ambitious merchant, moved to London, became Chairman of the East India Company and was created a Baronet. His sister married the eminent eighteenth-century lawyer, John Dunning, Lord Ashburton, remembered for his famous resolution that 'the power of the Crown has increased, is increasing, and ought to be diminished'. This Ashburton peerage expired with the Dunnings' son but Sir Francis Baring's younger son, Alexander, managed to have it revived in his favour in 1835. History has given the name of 'Ashburton' to the treaty that Alexander Baring concluded delimiting the frontiers of Canada and the United States of America.

The banking house of Baring Brothers looks after the finances of the royal family, and two of the five Baring peers, the present Lord Ashburton and his cousin the Earl of Cromer, are Knights of the Garter. Lord Ashburton has been Lord-Lieutenant of Hampshire and his son and heir, John Baring, incurred the wrath of the heritage lobby when he pulled down part of that great neo-classical monument in the county, The Grange. The present Earl of Cromer has had a highly distinguished career outside the confines of the family bank. It has included a spell as Ambassador in Washington during the Nixon administration and as Governor of the Bank of Engand during a testing time at the beginning of the Wilson years, when he displayed exceptional strength of character. The Earldom of Cromer was created for that great saviour of Egypt, Sir Evelyn Baring—or 'Over Baring' as he was unkindly called—who was one of the early recipients of the Order of Merit.

The 1st Lord Cromer restored Egypt's finances and was for many years the virtual ruler of that country. 'A man of decided mind, his view may be right or it may be wrong, but it is always definite and he is always determined to push it through', wrote Lord Milner about his fellow Empire-builder. 'It would be difficult to over-estimate what the work of England in Egypt owes to his sagacity, fortitude and patience'. His younger son and namesake, Evelyn Baring, followed in his father's footsteps as a distinguished proconsul in Africa and was made Lord Howick of Glendale as the wind of change was reaped on that continent.

Before going out to Egypt, the great Lord Cromer was secretary to one of his Baring cousins, the 2nd Lord Northbrook, an extremely able Viceroy of India. The Northbrook peerage was conferred upon a nephew of the 1st Lord Ashburton, Sir Francis Baring, who was described by a contemporary as a capable Chancellor of the Exchequer in time of difficulty.

The family bank itself was in serious difficulties in 1890 and the Governor of the Bank of England received information that, 'though the firm was solvent, there were not sufficient liquid assets to meet the liabilities'. The government stepped in and Barings was reconstructed as a joint stock company; four years later the advances made to the company from the guarantee fund set up to avert a catastrophe had been repaid. The senior partner at the time of the crisis was an elder brother of the great Lord Cromer, the 1st Lord Revelstoke, who resigned in 1890. The problems were attributed to imprudent commitments in South America, particularly Argentina.

The unfortunate Lord Revelstoke's sons included the writer Maurice Baring, author of *The Puppet Show of Memory* and *Have You Anything to Declare?* Highly popular earlier this century, his works were largely forgotten until recently when there has been something of a 'rediscovery'. A previously unpublished collection of divertingly whimsical letters (*Dear Animated Bust*) from the front in the First World War to Lady Juliet Duff has also helped put Maurice Baring back on the map.

The seat of the Revelstoke line of the Barings is a romantic Lutyens-designed castle on Lambay Island off the coast of County Dublin. The 3rd Lord Revelstoke bought the island to escape to with his beautiful young wife, the daughter of Pierre Lorillard, the first American to win the Derby. The story of their early life here inspired Julian Slade's lilting 1950s' musical, *Free as Air*.

The Rothschilds are, of course, another important banking dynasty that entered the peerage in the nineteenth century. Nathan Mayer Rothschild, a great-grandson of the Frankfurt founder of this great house, became the first person to be raised to the peerage while still professing the Jewish faith, when he was created Lord Rothschild in 1885. A few years earlier he had succeeded to his uncle's Baronetcy. As well as continuing to attend their offices in the City, the Rothschilds had at Tring in Hertfordshire and elsewhere long since adopted the habits of the traditional country squirearchy.

Other branches of the family built the extraordinary French Renaissance treasure-house at Waddesdon in Buckinghamshire — planting fully grown trees on the bare hillside — as well as Mentmore in the same county. The latter Victorian pile passed to the Earls of Rosebery who offered it intact at a bargain price to the government, but the opportunity was missed, the contents dispersed and the place is now in the hands of the disturbingly smooth followers of the Maharishi Mahesh Yogi.

The 1st Lord Rothschild, who was a considerable benefactor of charities, had a genuine love of the countryside — for all the jibes about the 'Jews at Tring' — and this love of natural history has been inherited by his descendants. The present Lord Rothschild is an eminent Cambridge zoologist and his sister Miriam, a Trustee of the Natural History Museum, is also a most distinguished scientist. Recognized as having one of the most outstanding brains in the country, Lord Rothschild served the Heath Cabinet as head of the so-called 'Think Tank' (the Central Policy Review staff).

Outside the peerage, the new baronets in the nineteenth century included the brewer and philanthropist Sir Thomas Fowell Buxton, who worked with Wilberforce to abolish slavery and with his own sister-in-law Elizabeth Fry to reform the prisons. This philanthropic and radical strain has cropped up frequently among the great Sir Thomas's descendants.

His wife was a Gurney and these two families belong to that formidable and constantly intertwined East Anglian cousinhood which also includes the Barclays, Birkbecks and others. Sometimes the cousinhood is called — disobligingly and not quite accurately — the 'Quaker Mafia'. The cousinhood had made their fortunes, on the whole, in banking and brewing, establishing landed dynasties in great profusion in the nineteenth century. Although few of the cousinhood's estates have really been large enough to put them into the 'magnate' class, such is their prosperity and their standing that they seem to belong more to the greater than to the lesser aristocracy.

Another family which entered the baronetage in the nineteenth century can certainly be said to be of greater antiquity and acreage than the Buxtons — that of the Derbyshire Sitwells. Small gentry in medieval times, this famous family gradually grew richer through enclosures in the Elizabethan period, through iron founding and the manufacture of nails in the seventeenth century and through the business activities of William Sitwell — the last of the original male line — whose fortune when he died in 1776 was estimated at the then enormous figure of £400,000.

William Sitwell's nephew and heir, Francis Hurt, a scion of another long-established Derbyshire family, then assumed the surname of Sitwell. Francis's son, born Sitwell Hurt and who thus became Sitwell Sitwell, was made a Baronet in 1808 and greatly enlarged the family seat, Renishaw Hall, just south of Sheffield. The family afterwards came near to ruin through extravagance and financial misfortunes, but later in the nineteenth century, during the long minority of the 4th Baronet, coal was discovered on the Renishaw estate and this made the Sitwells prosperous once again.

One of the proliferating branches of WH Smith, the
stationers, at Pembroke, 1905. The Viscountcy of Hambleden
was created in 1891 for the widow of WH Smith, the
Victorian politician.

Tring Park, Hertfordshire, seat of Nathan Mayer Rothschild,
the banker who was given a Barony in 1885 thus becoming
the first person to be raised to the peerage while still
professing the Jewish faith.

The 4th Baronet was the eccentric Sir George Sitwell, immortalized by the writings of his children, the great literary trio of Edith, Osbert and Sacheverell Sitwell. Sir George had a number of strange ideas for inventions, including such useful items as a musical toothbrush that played 'Annie Laurie' and a really tiny revolver for shooting at wasps. One of his odd fancies was to stencil Chinese blue willow-patterns on the white cows in the park at Renishaw so as to enhance the landscape, but the beasts took exception to this liberty. He also wrote various scholarly monographs on a bewildering range of highly idiosyncratic antiquarian subjects ('Lepers' Squints', 'Acorns as an Article of Medieval Diet' etc).

The gaunt poet Edith Sitwell was advised by Sir George to take up gymnastics—'nothing a young man likes so much as a girl who is good at the parallel bars', he told her. Although the children's recollections of their incorrigible father made hilarious reading—particularly Sir Osbert Sitwell's autobiography *Left Hand, Right Hand*—the far from endearing awkwardness of Sir George should not be underestimated. For instance, he let his wife go to prison rather than bail her out of debt. The children became adept at keeping out of harm's way; on one occasion, so as to avoid an aunt, Edith adapted herself into the shape of an armchair while her brothers covered her with a cloth and carried her upstairs in safety past this unsuspecting relation.

Evelyn Waugh recalls an occasion when he stood with Sir George Sitwell on the terrace at Renishaw, admiring the sunset. In the valley at their feet lay 'farms, cottages, villas, the railway, the colliery and the densely teeming streets of the men who worked there'. 'You see', said Sir George, looking towards the hills beyond, 'there is *no one* between us and the Locker-Lampsons.'

The Sitwell trio were once described by Cyril Connolly as 'an alternative Bloomsbury'. Over the years such figures as TS Eliot, William Walton and Dylan Thomas basked in their patronage and the extraordinary pale 'Plantagenet' face of Edith helped the young Cecil Beaton make his name as a photographer. Noel Coward sneered at them as 'two wiseacres and a cow', but the Sitwells undeniably achieved a tremendous impact on the cultural life of the country with their 'skirmishes and hand-to-hand battles against the Philistines'.

Osbert Sitwell, 'educated during the holidays from Eton' (as his *Who's Who* entry read), began life in the unlikely setting of the Grenadier Guards, who were agreeably tolerant of his individual foibles. Like his sister Edith (who was made a Dame), he never married and lived most of his later life in Italy. The only surviving member of the great trinity and now the holder of the family Baronetcy, the poet and writer Sir Sacheverell Sitwell, lives in Northamptonshire. The family seat of Renishaw is now the home of his son, Reresby.

Aubrey Buxton (now Lord Buxton of Alsa, a life peer) on
location in Africa in *Survival*, his pioneering wildlife
television programme for Anglia Television.

The baronets were lumped in with the peers in the pride of *Peerage* works of reference that flourished in the nineteenth century; but in the 1830s the Burke family of genealogists and heralds started up *A Genealogical and Heraldic History of the Commoners of Great Britain and Ireland, enjoying Territorial Possessions or High Rank, but uninvested with Heritable Honours*. This splendid title was soon changed to *Landed Gentry*, which has helped foster that fictitious division in the aristocracy between 'nobility' and 'gentry'. It was about now that some people became rather carried away in claiming that the untitled squirearchy tended to have longer descents and wider acres than the peers, who were cast as Tudor upstarts and Georgian borough-mongers.

In fact, the number of 'great commoner' families which have steadily refused titles through the centuries is smaller than these mid-Victorian eulogists would have one believe. Many of the examples usually cited are either families whose Catholicism kept them out of politics or else they are closely connected to peers. And some of the proud, untitled magnates whom these writers so much admired were elevated to the peerage later in the nineteenth century.

A case in point is provided by the Leghs of Lyme Park in Cheshire— a seat grander than the palaces of many Continental sovereign princes (now run by the National Trust). The family was granted this estate by Richard II after the Battle of Crecy; they fought at Agincourt, Waterloo and Inkerman. As an historian of the Leghs has recounted, 'one entertained Elizabeth's Essex, another went to the Tower for refusing to swear allegiance to William III, and a third was an Egyptologist in the age of Byron. And in almost every generation the pull of the past was strong . . .'.

It is all splendid stuff, but in 1892—at about the same time as Lyme's famous breed of mighty mastiffs died out—the 'commoner' status was removed when William Legh, a former politician and member of the Jockey Club, became Lord Newton. As even their family historian sagely reminds us, the Leghs were 'also practical people who dug for coal and prospered from the expansion of Wigan and Warrington over their Lancashire estates'.

A striking example of an untitled dynasty produced by the Industrial Revolution also comes from the north-west in the form of the Arkwrights, whose fortunes were founded by the great Sir Richard Arkwright. Born the thirteenth child of humble parents at Preston in Lancashire in 1732, he earned his living as a barber and an itinerant hair merchant until his invention of the spinning frame brought him great wealth and a knighthood as well as revolutionizing the cotton industry throughout the world. Sir Richard's son and namesake, who died in 1848, was popularly believed to be the richest commoner in England. This Richard Arkwright founded four landed dynasties; but, in common with most of the other comparative newcomers, the Arkwrights were among the first to sell up when times changed.

Lord Margadale: the hunting heir to a nineteenth-century
haberdashery fortune and formerly a bastion of the Tory
backbenches in the House of Commons as member of parliament
for Salisbury.

Perhaps the most remarkable Victorian who rose to 'great commoner' status from commerce was the haberdashery tycoon, James Morrison. This self-made draper was worth about £2 million when he died in 1857, owning estates in five English counties, as well as Islay in Scotland. A member of parliament who voted for the Reform Bill, Morrison was also a champion of the railways. Although a believer in 'small profits and quick returns', his interests were not confined to commerce. Indeed, like so many of the much maligned 'new men' of the nineteenth century, he was a man of taste who made a name for himself as a collector and patron of the arts.

Morrison's great-grandson is Lord-Lieutenant of Wiltshire and represented Salisbury in the House of Commons for many years, wielding much influence in his role as Chairman of the backbench 1922 Committee. This Tory stalwart, who also owns the Islay estate where he used to entertain leading Conservative politicians in the summer recess, was created Lord Margadale in 1965. Lord Margadale's two younger sons Charles and Peter are both members of parliament—one 'wet', one 'dry', according to political observers—and his daughter Mary has been Woman of the Bedchamber to the Queen since 1960.

In Edwardian times and even after the First World War (in which many families lost heirs), the British aristocracy continued to grow. The ranks of the wealthy were noticeably increased around the turn of the century by a cosmopolitan element. An influx of families of foreign origin—American, South African, Greek, German-Jewish—were, once again, comfortably assimilated. By 1939 (the year which marked the 'end of civilization' rather more conclusively than 1914) the peerage was half as numerous again as it had been in 1900.

Despite the popular belief that Lloyd George flogged peerages at a brisk rate, the notorious honours broking carried out by Maundy Gregory and others was limited—with one or two exceptions—to baronetcies and knighthoods. The cascade of new hereditary peerages between 1900 and 1965 was largely uninfluenced by the old doctrine of 'endowment', whereby a peer was expected to support the dignity with an estate of some substance.

And so the landless peer of slender means—a rare phenomenon before the present century—has become a familiar figure. Nevertheless, a considerable number of the hereditary peerages created in the modern age have gone to merchant princes as rich as or richer than the newly created peers of former times.

The nineteenth-century industrial recruits to the peerage had not, in fact, been all that numerous, but now the tycoons flocked into the peerage: Lever, the soap magnate, became Viscount Leverhulme; Pearson, the engineering contractor, Viscount Cowdray; Cayzer, the shipowner, Lord Rotherwick; Boot, of the 'Cash Chemists', Lord Trent (a peerage that is now extinct); Vestey, the refrigeration magnate, Lord Vestey; Borwick, of the baking and

The two founding fathers of ICI: Sir John Brunner, 1st Baronet
(*left*), and his partner, the brilliant chemist Dr Ludwig
Mond (*right*), father of the 1st Lord Melchett.

From cattle boat to 'county' in three generations: the
2nd Lord Melchett out shooting in Hampshire.

custard powders firm, Lord Borwick; Lawson Johnston, of Bovril, Lord Luke. And so on.

Then there have been the 'Press Barons'—the Harmsworths, the Berrys and the American Astors—a powerful new element in the twentieth-century peerage.

One of the most noteworthy ascents in the modern peerage was made by Rufus Isaacs, son of a Spitalfields fruit merchant, who started out in life as a cabin boy and went on to make his name as a lawyer. He became the first Jew to become Lord Chief Justice and Viceroy of India, and at the end of his stint in India he was made Marquess of Reading. His principal business appointment was his Presidency of Imperial Chemical Industries, a company started by the 1st Lord Melchett, whose daughter married the 2nd Marquess of Reading.

The foundations of ICI had been laid by Lord Melchett's father, Ludwig Mond, a German Jew who arrived in England on a cattle boat in 1862. A brilliant chemist, Mond ended up as a millionaire, but also achieved his ambition of being a public benefactor who had improved manufacturing processes and saved waste. Moreover, he left his great collection of old masters to the National Gallery.

Apart from his business activities at ICI, Alfred Mond, the 1st Lord Melchett, was a politician who achieved Cabinet rank and became an enthusiastic Zionist, serving as Joint Chairman (with Chaim Weizmann) of the Jewish Agency and as Chairman of the Economist Board for Palestine. The 2nd Baron, Henry Mond, followed his father into politics but sadly he never succeeded to the Chairmanship of ICI due to the heart troubles that were also to plague his son Julian (the 3rd Lord Melchett). Henry took to country life on the family estate in Bedfordshire, acting as a Master of Foxhounds; but the start of the Nazi holocaust was his personal road to Damascus. 'There are plenty of people to look after the English,' he said, 'there are so few to look after the Jews'. He then devoted himself to the Zionist cause. His wife Gwen was a celebrated hostess at their London house in Smith Square.

This tradition of entertaining was stylishly carried on by their daughter-in-law, Sonia, the wife of the 3rd Lord Melchett. After a frustrating career with the merchant banking house of Hill Samuel (which he helped set up), Julian Melchett took on the challenge of forming the British Steel Corporation. The pressures of this difficult job doubtless contributed to his tragically early death aged forty-eight.

The Labour politician Sir Richard Marsh, who worked with the late Lord Melchett, has described the latter's 'extraordinary charisma' as a mixture of 'a very hard stubborn streak and gentleness expressed by his half stammer: enormous strength of character and enormous charm'. Marsh thinks 'he was the most impressive man I ever met'.

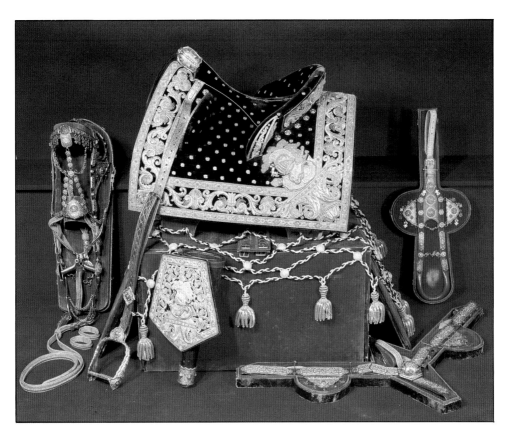

The sumptuous saddle, worked in gold thread, of the ill-fated Duke of Monmouth, Charles II's son by his first mistress Lucy Walters. Monmouth married the heiress of the Scotts of Buccleuch whose Border estates, including Bowhill (where the saddle is on display), have descended to the present Duke of Buccleuch.

Lord Montagu of Beaulieu (in the vintage motor-car) and his family painted by John Ward outside Palace House, the greatly enlarged monastic gatehouse which is the centre of the energetically commercialized leisure operation at Beaulieu near Southampton.

Kingston Lacy, Dorset, the late-seventeenth-century house designed
by Sir Roger Pratt and remodelled in the nineteenth century by Sir
Charles Barry, which the 'great commoner' family of Bankes
bequeathed to the National Trust in the early 1980s.

The Duke of Argyll, Chief of the Clan Campbell and Keeper of
the Great Seal of Scotland, in the Armoury Hall at Inveraray
Castle, with its fans of 'Brown Bess' muskets, Lochaber axes and
Highland broadswords. The Duke steadfastly restored the Castle
after a disastrous fire in 1975.

Sir Iain Moncreiffe of that Ilk, Baronet (1919–85), herald, genealogist, advocate, scholar, courtier, clubman and a singularly colourful chronicler of great British families, with his Irish wolfhound, O'Higgins.

Raeburn's celebrated portrait of the tartan-clad Highland Chief, MacDonell of Glengarry. As Sir Iain Moncreiffe has pointed out, Glengarry appears to have a knife and fork stuck in his stocking.

When he served in the last Labour Government, the present Lord Melchett became, at twenty-six, the youngest Minister since Pitt, winning plaudits for his work in Northern Ireland. A prominent 'Green' he is on record as being opposed to hereditary titles and 'privilege'; the obvious comment is that his own career has illustrated the advantages of such a system, for if he had not been a peer he would have been nowhere near ministerial office at such an age.

The great pottery family of Wedgwood was brought into the peerage in 1942 by a rather dim politician, Josiah Clement Wedgwood, who served in the first Labour government and chaired the committee that started the ball rolling on the projected book of the *History of Parliament*. The Wedgwoods, this multi-talented dynasty of academics, artists and writers, as well as of potters and politicians, are everyone's idea of a network of achievement. Although the estates and possessions of the family may never have placed it in the magnate class, its key role in what Lord Annan has described as the 'Intellectual Aristocracy'—Darwin, Huxley, Keynes—must surely give it the right to be included among the 'great' families, whatever criteria are applied.

Another dynasty of Cambridge University patricians, who also distinguished themselves in the British Raj, are the Butlers, long associated with Trinity College, Cambridge. One of the Masters of that college which this great family has provided once observed in a sermon that God was 'in some sense a Trinity man Himself'.

'As a result of marriages between his [of Josiah Wedgwood (1730–95), the great potter] descendants and leading members of the intelligentsia, he can claim to be the ancestor of some of the most brilliant people ever born in Britain, including Charles Darwin and Ralph Vaughan Williams.' So states *Debrett's Family Historian*. (Because the present writer is himself a descendant of Josiah—if a far from brilliant one—it was thought only fair to cite some independent evidence.)

The formidable concentration of brains that makes up the Darwin family has intermarried so many times with the Wedgwoods as to give rise to the saying that the Darwins were more Wedgwood that the Wedgwoods. The first to make such a marriage was Robert Darwin, the physician son of the eighteenth-century physiologist and poet, Erasmus Darwin, who married the daughter of the great Josiah Wedgwood himself. Their son was the eminent naturalist Charles Darwin, author of *The Origin of Species*, from whom all the later intellectual Darwins are descended.

Charles Darwin's sons included Sir George, Professor of Astronomy at Cambridge; Sir Francis, a botanist who was President of the British Association and his father's biographer; and Sir Horace, a civil engineer. The next generation produced the Cambridge physicist, Sir Charles Galton Darwin; Ruth Darwin, Senior Commissioner of the Board of Control for Lunacy; and Bernard Darwin, the writer and much-loved golf correspondent. More recent

Darwins, great-grandsons of Charles, include another crop of academics, a legal adviser to the Foreign Office and the painter Sir Robin Darwin, who was Principal of the Royal College of Art.

In her delightful *Period Piece*, Gwen Raverat gives us a picture of her eminent and highly eccentric Darwin uncles as seen through the eyes of a child. She tells of an occasion when another of Charles Darwin's sons, the engineer, economist and eugenist Major Leonard Darwin (author of a book on bimetallism, President of the Royal Geographical Society and sometime member of parliament), was on the platform at a political meeting. Absentmindedly, Uncle Lenny started rubbing his nose on the blotting paper. 'Do you find that soothing, Major Darwin?' the chairman asked him with mock solicitude.

It was said that one cousin 'made a vocation of invalidism' and certainly the Wedgwood-Darwin cult of unhealth could be indulged to excess. The Wedgwoods, in particular, have always taken themselves pretty seriously, failing to see the humorous side of things. Thus the Biblical quotation on the gravestone of an obscure member of the family who was accidentally shot by his gamekeeper read: 'Well done thou good and faithful servant.'

The founding father, Josiah Wedgwood, built up the most powerful and advanced industrial organization in England by skilfully exploiting the canal system. 'Owd Woodenleg' (as he was known in the works after an amputation) had the knack of getting things done in the most direct, uncomplicated manner. He was also a member of the Lunar Circle of Birmingham (or 'Lunatics' as his friend Erasmus Darwin called them) which included the scientists Watt and Priestley. The pottery lost much of its impetus after Josiah's demise, a death which was apparently hastened by his own dosage of laudanum. Then the family spread its political, social and artistic wings so that today no Wedgwood plays any active part in the pottery. This is perhaps just as well, considering the present company's attempts to demolish Barlaston Hall in Staffordshire — now happily frustrated by SAVE Britain's Heritage, which has restored the house for multiple occupation.

The most distinguished of the present generation of the family is, of course, the historian of the seventeenth century, CV Wedgwood. Dame Veronica is the sister of Sir John Wedgwood, 2nd Baronet, formerly Deputy Chairman of the pottery. Their father managed the old London North East Railway and was created a Baronet the day before his brother, Josiah Clement, became a peer.

An interesting twist in the twilight years of regular hereditary peerage creations was that the recipients sometimes measured up to the traditional county magnates of former times. For instance, Sir Ralph Assheton, a former Chairman of the Conservative Party Organization, who became Lord Clitheroe in 1955, heads a family that is one of the longest-established territorial dynasties in Lancashire. Similarly, among the last half-dozen or so

Erasmus Darwin, the eighteenth-century physiologist and poet, whose dining table had to be cut in a semi-circle to accommodate his stomach.

The great Victorian naturalist Charles Darwin (*left*) and his fellow botanists William Hooker and Charles Lyell who encouraged him to publish his controversial theory of evolution.

baronetcies occurs the Herefordshire family of Mynors who have been seated at Treago since the early fifteenth century.

Outside the modern peerage and baronetage, it is difficult to spot new landed dynasties establishing themselves on any major scale amid the speculators in agricultural land. A feature of our age is that—probably for the first time in history—the new rich no longer aspire to join the aristocracy. They seem to prefer, in the words of James Lees-Milne, 'a suburban villa with every "mod. con.", limitless Jaguars and mink to the cold rewards of territorial aggrandisement'.

CHAPTER VII

LOWLAND AND
HIGHLAND

SCOTLAND

THE OLD Gaelic-speaking tribal aristocracy of the Scottish Highlands or, for that matter, the French-orientated Lowland Scots aristocracy in the reigns of James V and Mary Stuart, cannot really be described as 'British'. It was not until 1603 when James VI of Scotland acceded to the English throne that the process began whereby the great Scottish families became great 'British' families. The Scots who came south to James's court were predominantly Lowlanders and this seventeenth-century 'Anglicization' had the effect of widening the gap between the broadly primitive Highlands and the more civilized Lowlands.

Indeed most of the Scottish peers in 1603 tended to come from Lowland families; the only prominent Highlander was the 7th Earl of Argyll, Chief of the Campbells, whose territory was in a part of the Highlands that abutted on to the Lowlands. It was this Earl's son, the Covenanting Marquis of Argyll, who was still posing a threat as an 'over-mighty subject' as late as the mid-seventeenth century.

When studying the Scots peerage, it is striking how uniform it seems compared with the English. The simple fact is that most of the present-day peers are descended in the male line from medieval families of some significance. Of the eighty-odd peers who hold peerages of Scotland — that is to say peerages created before the Act of Union with England in 1707 — over a quarter descend from families which held peerages in the Middle Ages and the ancestors of the majority of the rest were at least medieval magnates. Moreover, many Scotsmen who later received peerages of Great Britain (1707–1801) or of the United Kingdom (1801–1965) were also descended from the medieval aristocracy.

The most important of all Scottish families, the Royal House of Stuart, has several branches in the peerage at the present time, notably that of the Earls of Moray. They have a male Stuart descent, which is probably legitimate, from Robert, Duke of Albany, Regent of Scotland and son of the fourteenth-century monarch Robert II. They are also descended in the female line from Mary Queen of Scots' halfbrother, the Regent Moray, the eldest surviving bastard son of James V.

The rather devious Regent Moray had a somewhat chequered relationship with his halfsister. First he was her adviser and champion commander; then he was exiled for opposing her marriage to Lord Darnley, returning to Scotland after consenting to the messy murder of Rizzio at Holyrood, only to withdraw again before the Bothwell nuptials. He became Regent after Mary's abdication and successfully blocked her return before being bumped off by a Hamilton whose family he had wronged.

The Earldom of Moray passed by special remainder to his son-in-law, James Stuart (whose murder by the Gordons was lamented in the famous ballad The Bonny Earl of Moray) and thus down to the present Earl, whose principal seat, Darnaway Castle in Morayshire, incorporates the Regent's great hall. Two of the historic possessions at Darnaway are the Regent's skull, mounted as a drinking cup on silver acorns, and a contemporary portrait of the Bonny Earl's naked corpse showing its ghastly wounds. The present Earl's younger sister, Lady Arabella, is a cookery writer best known for *First Slice Your Cookbook* which was designed by her former husband Mark Boxer ('Marc', the cartoonist).

The premier Scots peer, the Duke of Hamilton, is, in the male line, a Douglas and holds the mighty medieval Douglas Earldom of Angus. The Hamiltons, whom he represents in the female line, were also medieval peers and, in the sixteenth century, they were very close to the throne. The 1st Duke of Hamilton was the unhappy favourite of Charles I who followed his master to the block. He was given the thankless task of enforcing the acceptance of the new Prayer Book in Edinburgh but when he tried to dissolve the Scottish Assembly he was merely ignored. His military adventures on behalf of the King were equally unsuccessful. One contemporary said of him: 'There is one good quality in this man, *viz.* that he was born and that God made him: and another, *viz.* that he is dead, and we must speak nothing but good of the dead'. This ineffective figure left no son and the Dukedom of Hamilton eventually passed by special remainder to his daughter, who married a Douglas.

The 4th Duke of Hamilton was also hardly mourned. He delayed taking up his post as Ambassador in Paris in 1712 to fight a duel in Hyde Park with Lord Mohun. The dispute, over an estate to which their respective wives were co-heiresses, was not settled with the customary decorum. The seconds started fighting each other and even an attendant footman was said to have

RECT SECVRVS.

James Stuart, 1st Earl of Moray, Mary Queen of Scots'
halfbrother who was Regent of Scotland from 1567 until
1570 when he was murdered. His skull, mounted as a
drinking cup on silver acorns, is preserved at the Stuart
family seat of Darnaway Castle, Morayshire.

joined in after his master Lord Mohun had been killed. The Duke himself was finished off by one of the seconds, a General Macartney, who was later convicted of manslaughter, though acquitted of murder. Within a week of this unseemly affair a contemporary was writing of the Duke: 'I assure you he has more friends at present than he ever had while alive.'

The duellist Duke's grandson, the 6th Duke of Hamilton, married Elizabeth Gunning, a celebrated Irish beauty for whom George III always had a soft spot. She later married the 6th Duke of Argyll and it was she who entertained Dr Johnson and studiously ignored Boswell when the pair visited Inveraray Castle, the Argyll family seat, during the Highland tour. Another famous beauty who married into the family of the Dukes of Hamilton was Nelson's 'bequest to the nation', the bawdy Emma, whose husband, Sir William Hamilton, was a nephew of the 4th Duke.

Later Dukes of Hamilton lived in semi-royal state at Hamilton Palace in Lanarkshire whose splendid pictures and furniture included part of the collection of the 10th Duke's father-in-law, William Beckford, the 'Caliph of Fonthill', one of the greatest patrons of the arts. In 1843 the 11th Duke of Hamilton made a royal marriage to the daughter of the reigning Grand Duke of Baden; and the 11th Duke's daughter married the reigning Prince of Monaco. Unfortunately the latter match was not a success: the 'English Princess', as Princess Mary was known by the Monégasques, regardless of the fact that she was Scottish, parted from her husband after only five months of marriage. However, she did produce a son and heir, the ancestor of the present Prince Rainier.

The family fortunes could not support the grandeur and extravagance of the nineteenth-century dukes and much of the contents of Hamilton Palace was sold by the 12th Duke in 1882. The Palace itself was tragically demolished in the 1920s, having suffered from coal-mining under the park. The present Duke, a motor-cycle enthusiast and former RAF officer, lives at Lennoxlove, a castle in East Lothian which was purchased by his father.

The late Duke's place in history came about in 1941 when Rudolf Hess, Hitler's deputy Führer, parachuted into Scotland and attempted to make contact with him, having met him at the Berlin Olympics before the war. One of the present Duke's brothers, Lord James Douglas-Hamilton, a former Tory member of parliament, wrote a book about Hess's strange mission. The late Duke's other cause for celebrity was being the first person to fly over the summit of Mount Everest. His brother holds the Douglas Earldom of Selkirk which came to him owing to the unusual way it descends.

In the male line, the Dukes of Hamilton are 'Red' Douglases. Their ancestor, a bastard son of the first of the Earls of Douglas (or 'Black' Douglases), obtained the Earldom of Angus in 1389. This 1st Earl of Angus married Princess Mary, daughter of Robert III but five years later he was taken prisoner by the English after the battle of Homildon Hill and died of the plague soon afterwards. His son and successor had revenge over the English at the battle of Piperdean in 1436. The 4th Earl of Angus also beat the English and increased the estates of this branch of the Douglases by helping to quash the rebellion of his kinsman, the last Earl of Douglas. A case, it was said, of the 'Red Douglas putting down the Black'.

The 5th 'Great' Earl of Angus, known as 'Bell-the-Cat', continued the territorial aggrandizement of the Red Douglases and held high office as Warden of the East Marches. However, he blotted his copybook at Flodden in 1513 by presuming to advise James IV against fighting this fatal battle with the English. This did not go down at all well with the King and the Great Earl left the field shortly before hostilities got under way. None the less, he bade his two sons remain there to do their duty. Both were killed with the King.

The Red Douglases became particularly powerful in the sixteenth century, when the Great Earl's grandson, the 6th Earl of Angus, married James IV's widow, Queen Margaret, sister of Henry VIII of England—a marriage shrewdly planned by Henry VII with an eye to the eventual unification. This marriage, however, was not to the liking of James V who had the 6th Earl and his kinsman forfeited, while the Earl's sister, Lady Glamis, was burned at the stake for witchcraft. After James's death, the 6th Earl recovered his titles and estates and the Douglases regained their influence. The 6th Earl's grandson, the pox-ridden Lord Darnley (son of the 6th Earl's only child, Margaret), became the consort of Mary Queen of Scots.

In the reign of Charles I, the 11th Earl of Angus rose to being Marquis of Douglas; and one of his younger sons married the heiress of the Hamiltons. When the 3rd Marquis, who was made Duke of Douglas, died in 1761, the Marquisate of Douglas and Earldom of Angus passed to his cousin, the 7th Duke of Hamilton, but the Douglas estates went to his sister's son. Thereby, however, hangs the celebrated saga of the 'Douglas Cause' when a lawsuit decided that the nephew really was his sister's son and not a child adopted by her in Paris as he was thought to have been. Doubt still remains as to the nephew's parentage, even though the verdict of the House of Lords enabled him to inherit the Douglas estates, which eventually passed to his granddaughter, who married the 11th Earl of Home.

The 12th Earl of Home duly took the surname of Douglas-Home which became well known when his politician grandson, the 14th Earl, renounced the Earldom on becoming Prime Minister in 1963. Sir Alec (or Lord Home of The Hirsel as he now is) still owns some of the Douglas lands in Lanarkshire, though the Home seat is The Hirsel in Berwickshire, where the family has long been established. One of the politician's brothers is the playwright William Douglas-Home, whose various works include a dramatic rendering of the Douglas Cause and an account of his time in prison for refusing to obey an order to shell a French village after the D-Day landings. Another brother of Sir Alec's was the ornithologist, Henry Douglas-Home, whose son, Charles, became the Editor of *The Times*.

A different branch of the Douglases, descended from a bastard son of the 2nd Earl of Douglas, is represented in the male line by the Marquis of Queensberry and in the female line by the Duke of Buccleuch. The head of this branch of the Black Douglases became Duke of Queensberry in 1683 after he had helped suppress the Covenanters.

The 1st Duke of Queensberry and his son were supporters of the 'Glorious Revolution' of 1688. 'The son', grumbled one contemporary, 'notwithstanding King Charles and King James's kindness to his father and family . . . was the first Scotsman that deserted over to the Prince of Orange, and from thence acquir'd the epithet (amongst honest men) of Proto-rebel.' Known as the 'Union Duke' for his championing of the Act of Union, the 2nd Duke of Queensberry was an enigmatic character. The historian of the Douglases maintained that 'the statesman who should undertake this formidable task had need not only of moral fortitude and conviction, but of personal courage'. However, Queen Anne never cared for him and was reluctant to restore him to high office after he had fallen from favour as an innocent victim of the so-called 'Scottish' or 'Queensberry' plot in 1704.

The Act of Union also indirectly caused a ghastly episode in the history of the Douglas family. The 'Union Duke' had an unhinged son who was kept locked up in a cell at Holyrood, but during the debates on the Union this dangerous Earl of Drumlanrig was left unguarded while the servants went out to see the riots in Edinburgh. He escaped from his confinement and fell upon a cookboy, who was turning the spit in the kitchen. After killing the wretched menial, Lord Drumlanrig then proceeded to truss the corpse up on the spit and roast it before the fire. Thankfully the 'cannibalistic idiot' (as he was known) had already been passed over in the entail of the Dukedom and the estates.

The 3rd Duke of Queensberry felt obliged to resign as Admiral of Scotland when his wife was 'forbid the Court' of George II. The spirited Duchess had transgressed by touting for subscriptions for the play *Polly* by her protégé, John Gray, at a 'Drawing-Room' (as royal receptions used to be known). A beautiful, warm-hearted and eccentric woman, Duchess Kitty was much loved by the wits of the day. She was certainly not lacking in wit herself. When Horace Walpole proposed a toast wishing that she 'might live to grow ugly', the Duchess replied, 'I hope, then, you will keep your taste for antiquities'.

The next Duke of Queensberry was the notorious rake known as 'Old Q' and 'The Star of Piccadilly'. He became a familiar sight in early nineteenth-century London as he ogled the girls from his vantage point on a balcony near Hyde Park Corner. In his youth, according to Wraxall, he 'nourished an ardent and a permanent passion, during several years' for Frances, the

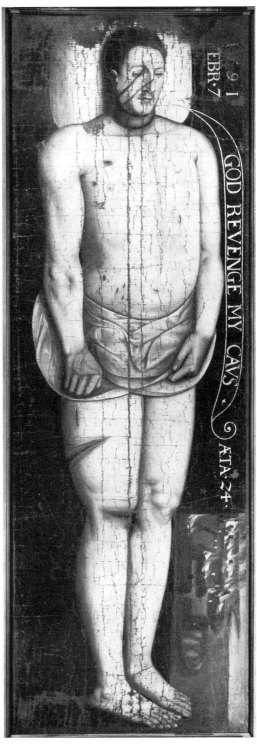

A contemporary portrait at Darnaway shows the ghastly
wounds on the naked corpse of the 2nd Earl of Moray
(celebrated through the ballad as 'the Bonny Earl') who
was slashed to death by the Gordons in 1591.

daughter of Thomas Pelham, the Prime Minister. 'But her father, considering him a nobleman of dissipated habits, character and fortune, interdicted their union.' Before settling in the centre of London to enjoy the passing show, Old Q spent most of his time at Queensberry House on the river at Richmond. 'What is there to make so much of in the Thames,' he said. 'I am quite tired of it—there it goes, flow, flow, flow always the same.' By the turn of the century, as Wraxall relates, his person had become 'a ruin, but not so his mind. Seeing only with one eye, hearing very imperfectly only with one ear, nearly toothless, and labouring under multiplied infirmities, he possessed all his intellectual faculties, including his memory. Never did any man retain more animation, or manifest a sounder judgement'.

Upon the death of this raddled old bachelor in 1810 ('of a severe flux') the Dukedom and the Marquisate of Queensberry went in different directions. The Dukedom of Queensberry went to the 3rd Duke of Buccleuch (whose grandmother was the 2nd Duke of Queensberry's daughter); while the Marquisate of Queensberry went to a Douglas cousin.

Of the subsequent Marquises of Queensberry, the best known is the late-Victorian sportsman who gave his name to the 'Queensberry Rules' which govern boxing—though it seems doubtful whether he really had much to do with them. A noted amateur pugilist himself, he once knocked out a 'gigantic cowboy' in California. He is, of course, chiefly remembered as the over-bearing father of the litigious poet Lord Alfred ('Bosie') Douglas, with whom Oscar Wilde formed his fatal friendship. The dramatist once told his servant that the Marquis was 'the most infamous brute in London'.

Our picture of the 'Screaming Scarlet Marquis' may be over-influenced by the unfavourable light in which he was cast by Oscar and Bosie. In his favour, for instance, it can be pointed out that he published a meditation in blank verse entitled 'The Spirit of the Matterhorn' and Rebecca West has drawn attention to his sympathetically liberal championing of the rights of atheists in the Victorian age. Curiously enough, both he and his eldest son died in shooting accidents. The *Evening Herald* states with regard to the father, that 'in sporting circles a belief is expressed that the death was not accidental; he had lately sustained heavy losses'.

The 11th Marquis of Queensberry married a musical comedy actress; but it was by his second wife, a painter, that he became father of the present Lord Queensberry, Professor of Ceramics at the Royal College of Art and proprietor of the Reject China Shops. The present Marquis no longer has a house in Scotland, though he availed himself of the more considerate Scots law on legitimacy when he succeeded in having his son Sholto, who had been born out of wedlock, recognized by his heir. In England, although Sholto would have been legitimized by his parents' subsequent marriage, he would not have been eligible to inherit the title: the Earl of Norbury, for instance, has in fact an elder brother.

'Old Q', the 4th Duke of Queensberry (1729–1810) known as
the 'Goat of Piccadilly', on the town, as captured by
Rowlandson. Wordsworth described the Duke as 'Degenerate
Douglas! Oh, the unworthy lord . . .'.

The Duke of Buccleuch—as we saw in the chapter on 'Royal Favourites'—represents an illegitimate Stuart line, being descended from the dashing Duke of Monmouth, Charles II's son by his first mistress, Lucy Walters. A romantic story is told, incidentally, of a nineteenth-century Duke of Buccleuch showing Queen Victoria evidence of Lucy's marriage to the King and then throwing it on the fire.

The erratic Monmouth was constantly in the thick of schemes to gain the throne for himself and even went so far as to join in the Rye House Plot to assassinate both his father and his uncle, the future James II. On the latter's accession in 1685, the wayward Duke, who had been banished abroad, landed in the West Country to lead a rebellion. He got as far as Somerset, being proclaimed 'King Monmouth' at Taunton, before his followers were savagely defeated on Sedgemoor by his uncle's army—one of whose commanders was the future Duke of Marlborough.

Monmouth married the heiress of a long-established Border family, the Scotts of Buccleuch, and took her name. His wife, Anna (described by the diarist John Evelyn as 'one of the wittiest and craftiest of her sex'), had inherited her father's Earldom of Buccleuch and was created Duchess of Buccleuch on her marriage. Although Monmouth's own titles were forfeited on his execution in 1685, his wife's were not. They have duly descended, together with the Scott estates, to the present Duke of Buccleuch, who, but for the forfeiture, would also be Duke of Monmouth.

The 3rd Duke of Buccleuch, a patron of literature, not only came into the Douglas Dukedom of Queensberry, together with the estates that went with it, but also married the eventual heiress of the English Dukes of Montagu. This match brought the Buccleuchs yet another ducal estate. All this meant that in the nineteenth century the Montagu-Douglas-Scotts were the wealthiest family in the British peerage with an income of more than £200,000 a year from their 460,000 acres.

Part of the Montagu property eventually passed to a younger son of the 5th Duke of Buccleuch, who became the 1st Lord Montagu of Beaulieu. The second peer of this line was a celebrated pioneer of motoring and aviation. On coming down from Oxford young Montagu trained as a mechanic in the workshops of the London and South-Western Railway where he also qualified as a train driver. The founder of *Car Illustrated*, the 2nd Lord Montagu took Edward VII on his first motor drive, becoming the first to drive a car into Palace Yard.

The present Lord Montagu of Beaulieu has inherited his father's interest in motor-cars, running the famous motor museum on his estate in Hampshire, and he has played a leading part in the development of the heritage lobby. He founded the Historic Houses Association, a sort of trades union for country house owners, and is now chairman of 'English Heritage', otherwise the Historic Buildings and Monuments Commission.

The rest of the combined heritage of the Scotts, Douglases and Montagus has descended more or less intact to the present paraplegic Duke of Buccleuch. A former Tory member of parliament, the Duke manages to lead an active public life though confined to a wheelchair following a riding accident. As well as other smaller country houses, the Duke owns four magnificent seats: the spectacular Baroque Queensberry Castle of Drumlanrig in Dumfriesshire; the glorious late-seventeenth-century Boughton, seat of the Montagus, in Northamptonshire; the mainly nineteenth-century Bowhill on the original Buccleuch lands in Selkirk; and the principal Buccleuch mansion, Dalkeith, near Edinburgh. Although Dalkeith is now empty of furniture, the other three houses between them contain one of the finest privately owned art collections in Europe. A few years ago the present Duke's eldest son, the Earl of Dalkeith, revealed that even the Buccleuch estates, though among the largest and most efficiently run territorial empires in Europe, were having difficulty in finding something of the order of the £¾ million required to repair their four seats.

As well as being descended from Charles II, the Duke of Buccleuch is closely connected to the present royal family through being a nephew of Princess Alice, Duchess of Gloucester (his father's sister). Even more closely associated with the royal family is the Earl of Strathmore, great-nephew of Queen Elizabeth the Queen Mother—a relationship which gives him a unique position among the Scottish peers. And long before Lady Elizabeth Bowes-Lyon married the future George VI, the Strathmores were one of the most famous of the great families of Scotland.

Such is the distinction of the Strathmores' long and eventful history, that it was jokingly suggested that when Lady Elizabeth (known, prophetically, as 'Princess' when she was a girl) finally agreed to marry the second son of George V, she was rather marrying beneath her. The family seat, Glamis Castle, is everyone's idea of a Scottish castle, with its massive tower and cluster of pointed turrets. It is notorious for the proverbial 'Monster' (which some say was merely a lunatic Lyon) which is said to inhabit a secret room in the Castle and to constitute the dread secret allegedly passed from generation to generation with the title.

Glamis was originally a hunting lodge of the medieval Scots kings to whom it belonged, until Robert II granted it to his son-in-law, Sir John Lyon—grandfather of the 1st Lord Glamis—in 1372. The Castle and lands reverted to the Crown for a period in the sixteenth century, having been seized by James V at the same time as he had the widowed Lady Glamis burned at the stake in Edinburgh on a trumped-up charge of practising sorcery against him. When the King died, Glamis was restored to the unfortunate lady's son, the 7th Lord Glamis, who had been condemned to death with his mother but reprieved on account of his tender years.

In the seventeenth century, the family obtained the Earldom of Strathmore and Kinghorne. The family name became Bowes-Lyon, after the Strathmores had inherited the estates of the wealthy Durham family of Bowes, whose heiress married the 9th Earl of Strathmore in 1767. In the time of his son, the 10th Earl, the young Walter Scott came to Glamis and noted that in spite of the 'truth of history' (for the king murdered here was not Duncan, but his grandfather Malcolm II), 'the whole night scene in Macbeth's Castle rushed at once upon me and struck my mind more forcibly than even when I have seen its terrors represented by John Kemble and his inimitable sister [Mrs Siddons]'.

The wife of Sir John Lyon, the progenitor of the Strathmores, was the youngest of Robert II's daughters by his first marriage. One of her elder sisters married Sir Thomas de la Haye, ancestor of an even more historic Scottish family, the Hays, Earls of Erroll. Sir Thomas de la Haye's father became hereditary High Constable of Scotland, an office which the present Earl of Erroll still holds, making him the first subject in Scotland after the Blood Royal, with precedence over every other peer regardless of rank. Long before they were made Earls of Erroll in 1452, and for many centuries afterwards, the de la Hayes or Hays played a leading part in Scottish affairs.

The present Earl's grandfather, the 22nd Earl of Erroll, met a violent end more suited to a Scots noble of the sixteenth than of the twentieth century. He was murdered in Kenya during the Second World War and was believed at the time to have been the victim of a *crime passionnel*. An elderly Cheshire Baronet, Sir 'Jock' Delves Broughton, was acquitted of the deed in a trial that caused a major sensation even though it happened in the middle of the Second World War and has recently been filmed as *White Mischief*.

Upon the death of the murdered Earl although the Erroll Earldom went to his daughter, 'Puffin' (then the wife of Sir Iain Moncreiffe of that Ilk, the herald), the Barony of Kilmarnock went to his younger brother.

In fact since the sixteenth century the Earls of Erroll have not been Hays by male descent, though bearing that surname. The 15th Earl who succeeded his Jacobite great-aunt, was previously Lord Boyd, son of the last Earl of Kilmarnock. The Earldom was forfeited when Lord Kilmarnock was attainted after the '45 rebellion and beheaded on Tower Hill, together with Lords Lovat and Balmerino — the last three peers in British history to be executed for high treason.

Hogarth has given us a famous painting of the gross 'Old Fox' Lovat on his way to execution. 'You'll get that nasty head of yours chopped off, you ugly old Scotch dog', yelled a crone in the crowd. 'I believe I shall, you ugly old English bitch', riposted Lord Lovat.

The present Lord Lovat, who became famous as a commando leader in the Second World War, has the rare distinction of being a Highland chief as well as a member of the old Scots peerage. In the South African War his father raised and commanded the Lovat Scouts, a regiment composed of his

Lady Elizabeth Bowes-Lyon (or 'Princess' as she was
prophetically known as a girl) with her brother David
and their dancing master, 1909.

own clansmen. But while, as chiefs of the Clan Fraser, they are known by the Gaelic title of *MacShimi*, and while they have plenty of Celtic blood in their veins from maternal ancestors of Highland stock, the Lords Lovat are, in the male line, Norman-French, like so many other Scottish aristocrats. For two or three centuries after settling in Scotland, the Frasers lived entirely in the Lowlands — indeed several Lowland branches of the family exist to this day.

A roll-call of the other great families in the old peerage of Scotland would certainly have an overwhelmingly strong Lowland flavour. Apart from the Hamiltons, Douglases, Homes and Scotts, such a list would have to include the families of Graham, Gordon, Kerr, Leslie, Lindsay, Erskine and Maitland. However, the hackneyed line in the song 'Bonnie Dundee', 'If they're Lords in the South, there are Chiefs in the North', is misleading, in that there are Lowlands — and lords for that matter — in the north as well as in the south. Thus, Caithness, the most northerly county of all, is predominantly 'Lowland' and the Sinclairs have been Earls of Caithness since 1455. The present Lord Caithness is a junior minister at the Home Office.

The Grahams produced the great Marquis of Montrose, that Cavalier who came so near to the Renaissance concept of the 'Complete Man'. Unfortunately this romantic personage was anything but complete after the Roundheads had sentenced him to have his head and limbs distributed among the the principal cities of Scotland; but Charles II had his remains reassembled and reburied in state at St Giles's Cathedral, Edinburgh.

For centuries the Grahams had been the chief marcher lords of what is sometimes called Scotland's 'northern' border, the fertile strip along the northern shore of the Forth separating the hills from the Highlands. Montrose's ancestors were in the peerage from 1445 and Earls of Montrose from 1505; he himself was made a Marquis and his great-grandson became a Duke. The present Duke, sometime member of Ian Smith's Cabinet, lives in Zimbabwe, but his son and heir still lives in Scotland.

Among the great Montrose's staunchest supporters were the Ogilvys, later Earls of Airlie, whose lands in Angus lay not far from his own. A sixteenth-century feud between the Ogilvys and the Gordons led to the rebellion of George Gordon, 4th Earl of Huntly. This powerful figure, reputed to have been the richest subject in Scotland, was so outraged by his defeat at the hands of the royal army that he promptly died of apoplexy. His embalmed corpse was duly arraigned before Mary Queen of Scots and her parliament in Edinburgh, found guilty and attainted. Ironically, this rebel against a Catholic queen was himself the leader of the Catholic party in Scotland.

The Gordons had been Earls Huntly since 1445 and the apoplectic Earl's father, who commanded a wing of the Scots army at Flodden but escaped the slaughter, was the first Huntly to bear the celebrated sobriquet of 'Cock o' the North'. The family later became Marquises and then Dukes, but the

Glamis Castle, Forfarshire, the ancestral seat of the
Lyons, and everybody's idea of a Scotch stronghold.

Dukedom has not survived. The present Lord Huntly, an educationalist and Sotheby's representative, is the Premier Marquis of Scotland. He has imaginatively restored the family seat of Aboyne Castle, removing the Victorian accretions.

The other Gordon in the present-day peerage, the Marquis of Aberdeen, is traditionally descended from a branch of the Huntlys. These Gordons produced the upright Victorian Prime Minister Earl of Aberdeen, who led the coalition government which was blamed for the mismanagement of the Crimean War; and his grandson, the Governor-General of Canada and Viceroy of Ireland, who was promoted to a Marquisate.

Paramount among the very few Highland chiefs in the old peerage is the Duke of Argyll, Chief of the most powerful clan of all, the Campbells, whose family history is so much a part of the history of Scotland. His ancestors became Earls in the fifteenth century, rising to a Marquisate in the seventeenth century and finally to a Dukedom in 1701. The careers of the Earls of Argyll show how the Campbells have long been of national, as well as local, importance. The 1st Earl was an envoy to France and Lord Chancellor of Scotland; he also held the office of Master of the Royal Household (which eventually became hereditary and is now vested in the present Duke of Argyll). The 5th and 6th Earls of Argyll also became Lord Chancellors whereas the 3rd Earl had been Lord Justice General of Scotland — another important office that became, for a considerable period, hereditary — as well as Lord Warden of the Marches. The 2nd Earl was killed commanding the Highlanders at the Battle of Flodden; the 4th Earl was to the fore at the Battle of Pinkie. Loyal supporters of the Stuarts, the Earls of Argyll worked long and hard to bring the Western Highlands and islands under the government.

The 'Grim' 7th Earl of Argyll, however, was formally declared a rebel and traitor at the Market Cross in Edinburgh in 1621 shortly after he had embraced the Catholic faith. Such a conversion might seem unexpected as in his younger days he had fought, unsuccessfully, against the Catholic rebel Earls of Erroll and Huntly at the battle of Glenlivat. The reason was that he had married a Catholic lady, Anne Cornwallis, a writer of some distinction. Happily the Market Cross sentence was reversed, but he had already been obliged to make the estates over to his son, who once tried to poison him.

It is hardly surprising that the son, who became the 1st Marquis of Argyll and leader of the bigoted Covenanting party that sought to impose religious control on the country, was not exactly the apple of his father's eye. The paternal view expressed to James VI (and I) was that here was 'a man of craft and subtlety and falsehood, and can love no man; and if ever he finds it in his power to do you a mischief he will be sure to do it'. Described as a small, wiry, squinting, blue-eyed, red-haired man, with a high forehead and hooked nose, he became the deadly foe of the romantic Montrose. Although he crowned Charles II at Scone after the execution of Charles I, the

SIMON LORD LOVAT,

From the Original by Hogarth.

TAKEN A FEW HOURS BEFORE HIS EXECUTION FOR HIGH TREASON

Hogarth's portrait of the Jacobite Simon Fraser, 11th
Lord Lovat, who was beheaded on Tower Hill, 1547: the
last peer of the realm to be axed.

Marquis of Argyll was executed at the Restoration on account of his Cromwellian collaboration.

The squint-eyed Marquis's son ('King Campbell') was sentenced to a similar fate for refusing to subscribe to the Test Act, but this first Colonel of the Scots Guards managed to escape from Edinburgh Castle disguised as a page holding up the train of his stepdaughter. However, in 1685, his head rolled at the Market Cross, just as his father's had before him.

The death of King Campbell's son, the 1st Duke of Argyll, occurred in a more agreeable fashion 'in the arms of his whore'. A vigorous anti-Jacobite and supporter of the Glorious Revolution, he was given a Dukedom by William III. It was in his time as Chief that the Clan Campbell legendarily disgraced themselves by dispatching thirty-eight Macdonalds while enjoying that Clan's hospitality at Glencoe.

As for the 2nd Duke of Argyll, Horace Walpole considered 'that posterity will probably interest themselves very slightly in the history of his fortunes'. None the less, he was one of the first two Field Marshals ever to be appointed in the British army and the first Knight of the Thistle also to receive the Garter. Whether he lived up to the Garter's ideals of chivalry is another matter: Lady Louisa Stuart complained that he had 'the most illiberal contempt for women'. Of the 3rd Duke, Lady Louisa noted that he was 'interested in philosophical experiments, mechanics and natural history'; though Lord Hervey felt he had 'no attachment but to his own interest'. Inheriting the Argyll estates at the age of sixty, this Duke set to planning a new seat at Inveraray on Loch Fyne which was completed in magnificent style by another Field Marshal in the family, the 5th Duke, who entertained Johnson and Boswell at the Castle in 1773.

Just over a hundred years later, in the time of the 8th Duke of Argyll, a Liberal politician, Inveraray was the scene of a conflagration; and a century later again, in 1975, the Castle was once more gutted by fire. Although most of the splendid contents were saved, serious structural damage was suffered in this later fire. Nothing daunted, the present Duke put matters to rights with laudable swiftness, even if at frightening cost to the estate.

The 9th Duke of Argyll, who was Governor-General of Canada, married Queen Victoria's daughter, Princess Louise, but this childless union was not a success. It has been suggested that the Duke's tastes lay in another direction. While the couple lived mostly apart, there was no formal separation; very different was the long-drawn-out divorce of the 11th Duke from his third wife—the much-photographed Margaret Whigham—to which the newspapers devoted so much space in the early 1960s. The present Duke's journalist halfsister was briefly the wife of Norman Mailer.

Among the various cadet lines of the Argylls in the peerage are the Campbells, Earls Cawdor. The story goes that in 1498 the posthumous daughter of the 8th Thane of Cawdor was abducted by the Campbells and

The present Lord Lovat, with his wife, the former Rosamond Delves Broughton (only daughter of Sir 'Jock' Delves Broughton, one of the central figures in the Kenyan *cause célèbre* immortalized in the film *White Mischief*), after an investiture at Buckingham Palace in 1942 when he was awarded the DSO and MC for his Commando exploits. The 24th Chief of Clan Fraser (*MacShimi*), he feuded with his brother officer Evelyn Waugh who portrayed him as Trimmer, the hairdresser and bogus war hero, in his trilogy *Sword of Honour*.

Two 'younger sons'. Angus Ogilvy, younger brother of the present Earl of Airlie whose once-Jacobite family eventually became staunch servants of the House of Windsor. Mr Ogilvy married Princess Alexandra of Kent in 1963. He is being pointed at by Francis Sitwell, younger son of Sir Sacheverell Sitwell, Baronet, himself the youngest of the famous Sitwell siblings.

The 7th Earl of Argyll, known as 'Archibald the Grim',
who was defeated by the Catholic rebel Earls of Erroll
and Huntly in 1594 at Glenlivat but later became a Catholic
himself.

The squint-eyed 1st Marquis of Argyll crowning Charles II
at Scone on New Year's Day 1650. The Covenanting Lord
Argyll was however executed at the King's Restoration
for having collaborated with Cromwell.

married to a younger son of the 2nd Earl of Argyll; a union which, as was often the case with this sort of caper, worked out rather well. According to legend, the 3rd Thane had a dream about a new castle at Cawdor whereby he was instructed to 'let a donkey, laden with gold, wander about the chosen area; wherever the donkey lay down to rest in the evening there he should build his house'. Doubtless to the Thane's chagrin, the animal parked himself beneath a hawthorn tree. And to this very day, in the centre of the ground-floor chamber of the tower-house at Cawdor there rises the trunk of an old hawthorn.

The 1st Lord Cawdor, who also inherited sizeable Welsh estates, has a place in history through his association with the last invasion of Britain, for it was he who accepted the surrender of Napoleon's muddled expeditionary force at Fishguard in 1797. The present 'Thane' describes his family history as 'Good plain cooking with an occasional pinch of red pepper'; but in the last century this branch of the Campbells can claim three VCs, fifteen DSOs and three Croix de Guerre. The Earls (and former Marquises) of Breadalbane, who used to be very large landowners in Perthshire and Argyll, are another offshoot of the main Campbell line.

Because comparatively few Scots were made peers after the Act of Union, Scotland can probably boast of more territorial magnates outside the peerage — with or without baronetcies — in proportion to its size than England. Pride of place must, of course, go to Cameron of Lochiel, whose forebears were virtually independent potentates until the seventeenth century and who still commands a semi-regal awe in the Highlands.

As might be expected, the Cameron history is a long chronicle of clan warfare, bloodshed and deeds of valour. The 8th Chief fought alongside David II at the Battle of Halidon Hill; the 13th Chief was beheaded in 1547; the 17th Chief, Sir Ewen Cameron, when fighting against the troops of the Cromwellian, General Monck, killed an Englishman by biting his throat. The 18th Chief was attainted after coming out on the side of the Pretender in the '15 rebellion; just as his son was attainted for joining Bonnie Prince Charlie with 800 clansmen in the '45. A younger son of the 18th Chief was the last person to suffer death as a Jacobite, being arrested and executed in 1753.

The 21st Chief of the Camerons was allowed to return to Scotland from abroad and used his influence to raise Lochiel men for the service of the British government. And so his son and successor was restored to the family estates. The present Chief is a Knight of the Thistle, as his father was before him, the first Knight ever to be nominated who was not either a peer or a baronet. As a further indication of the standing of his family, both the present Chief's father and grandfather married dukes' daughters. Sir Donald Cameron of Lochiel, whose little granddaughter was one of the bridesmaids to the Princess of Wales at her wedding in 1981, is Lord-Lieutenant of

Cawdor Castle, Nairn, with its great tower built by the
then Thane of Cawdor in the fifteenth century, and late seventeenth-
century additions. The Castle is now the home of the 6th Earl of Cawdor.

Duart Castle, by the Sound of Mull, the stronghold of
Lord Maclean, 27th Chief of the Clan, a former Chief
Scout and Lord Chamberlain.

Iverness-shire, Colonel of the Lovat Scouts and a Crown Estates Commissioner. Only a few peers have larger estates than his own. Indeed Lochiel can be said to be almost unique among the long-established landed families in owning more land than was held by his predecessor of a century ago—the family estates having now increased to some 130,000 acres.

Other Highland Chiefs, no longer holding such broad acres as Lochiel, but with names as proud as his, include MacGregor of MacGregor, Maclean of Duart, Macdonald of Clanranald and Macdonell of Glengarry. The family history of most of these chiefs is broadly similar to that of the Camerons: clan warfare and family rivalry until the seventeenth century; Jacobitism in the eighteenth; service of the British Crown in more recent times. Clanranald and Glengarry may no longer be landed at all, but in Scotland the size of one's estate is of less importance than the length of one's pedigree. None the less, the present MacLeod of MacLeod still lives in his ancestral castle of Dunvegan on Skye—possibly the oldest inhabited castle in Scotland—and the present Maclean of Duart also inhabits an ancient castle, Duart on the Isle of Mull. A former Chief Scout of the Commonwealth, the latter is now Lord Chamberlain to the Queen and a life peer as Lord Maclean. He also holds the oldest of the two Maclean Baronetcies, which dates back to the time of Charles I, the more recent one having been conferred in 1957 on his adventurous kinsman, the soldier, politician and writer, Sir Fitzroy Maclean.

Many Lowland lairds can also produce equally impressive pedigrees, such as the Moncreiffes of that Ilk, who may very likely have held the lands of Moncreiffe near the City of Perth for 1,500 years, though they cannot trace their ancestry with certainty beyond Sir Matthew of Moncrieffe, who was living in 1248. The colourful writer and genealogist Sir Iain Moncreiffe of that Ilk, 11th Baronet, who died in 1985, succeeded his cousin who was burnt with the House of Moncreiffe in 1957. Recent figures in the family tree have ranged from a rancher in Wyoming to a translator of Proust.

Those lairds or chiefs who were not peers by the time of the Union tended to stay as they were, or at any rate did not rise above the rank of baronet. One of the few Scottish territorial magnates to be made a peer under the Georges or later was Sir Alexander Macdonald of Macdonald and Sleat who, like his father, the Chief at the time of the '45, was a supporter of the British government. His descendant, the present Lord Macdonald, Chief of Clan Donald, an hotelier on the Isle of Skye, still holds this Irish Barony conferred upon Sir Alexander in 1776.

Several families in the old peerage of Scotland rose to higher British titles after the Act of Union. For instance, the Crichton-Stuarts owe their Marquisate to the much maligned 3rd Earl of Bute, George III's unpopular Prime Minister—the last example of that extinct species, 'the royal favourite'. Another expatriate Scot who made good in London was the advocate, 'Silver-tongued' Murray, a younger son of the 5th Viscount Stormont, who

John Murray, 1st Marquis of Atholl, Keeper of the Privy
Seal, who 'played a trimming and shuffling part' in the
'Glorious Revolution' of 1688 which replaced James II
by William III. In Macaulay's view, Atholl was 'the
falsest, most fickle, the most pusillanimous of mankind'.

became Lord Chief Justice and Earl of Mansfield. (This branch of the Murrays is an offshoot of the great Dukes of Atholl.) And the Hopes eventually became Marquises of Linlithgow through the 7th Earl of Hopetoun, first Governor-General of Australia. His son, the 2nd Marquis of Linlithgow was Viceroy of India.

Out of the vast number of hereditary peers whose titles were created between 1707 and 1965, no more than about fifty can be counted as Scottish. Most of the Scots who obtained peerages from 1707 onwards were men of solid achievement. Some of them were of ancient lineage, such as Sir Gilbert Elliot, Governor-General of India and 1st Earl of Minto, who was the scion of a Border dynasty founded in the fifteenth century by Robert Elwald, squire to the 'Great' Earl of Angus. Others came from families of more recent origin.

The Sassenach prejudice against the self-made successful Scot in the eighteenth century is illustrated by the career of Sir Lawrence Dundas, ancestor of the Marquis of Zetland. Like so many successful Scots, Dundas was, however, the cadet of an 'old' family. He built up a fortune of between £600,000 and £800,000 as Commissary to the troops during the Seven years War, built up a parliamentary 'interest' and tried hard to obtain his 'favourite point', a peerage. But at his death in 1781 he was no more than a Baronet. It was not until 1794 that his son, Sir Thomas Dundas, was made Lord Dundas; his grandson rose to being Earl of Zetland in 1838 and the 3rd Earl became a Marquis in 1892 at the end of his stint as Lord-Lieutenant of Ireland. A younger son of the present Marquis (who is seated in Yorkshire), Lord David Dundas, made his name as an actor in the film *Prudence and the Pill* and later wrote a successful pop jingle about jeans.

It was Sir James Barrie who observed that there were few finer sights than a Scotsman on the make, and the nineteenth century saw a goodly number of them establishing dynasties, including some great industrialists such as the Tennants and the Colvilles, and the merchant princes of India and China like the Jardines. Again, the Colvilles, Lords Clydesmuir, of the steel firm, are cadets of the ancient landed aristocracy, being descended from Sir Robert Colville, a fifteenth-century Laird of Ochiltree, and also the ancestors of the Lords Colville of Culross. Sir John Colville, the courtier and Churchillian aide, was a member of the latter branch.

However, the pedigree of Lord Tweedsmuir is surprisingly short, going back no further than his great-grandfather, a nineteenth-century solicitor and banker at Peebles. The peerage was conferred on John Buchan, Governor-General of Canada and also, of course, a rattling good yarn-spinner.

Sir Charles Tennant a wealthy Glasgow chemical manufacturer founded a family which has been prominent in fashionable artistic and intellectual society ever since the 1880s, when his daughters—including the incorrigible Margot, afterwards wife of the Prime Minister, Herbert Henry Asquith—were leading spirits in the coterie known as 'the Souls'. The present Lord

Sir Walter Scott, as portrayed by Raeburn, whose assiduous
romancing did so much to revive Scotch traditions in the
nineteenth century.

In the eighteenth century, Cyril Connolly observed in *Enemies of Promise* (1938), his Eton contemporary Lord Dunglass might have been the sort to become Prime Minister. Later in the twentieth century he did, having disclaimed the Earldom of Home. Here, as Sir Alec Douglas-Home, he sets off from Downing Street in October 1963 to see the Queen.

A group photograph taken after the wedding of Princess Louise of Wales and the Duke of Fife, 27 July 1889. From left to right: (*standing*) Princess Victoria of Wales; the Duke of Fife; Princess Louise, Duchess of Fife; Princess May of Teck (later Queen Mary); Princess Marie Louise of Schleswig-Holstein; Countess Feodora Gleichen; (*seated*) Princess Maud of Wales; Countess Helena Gleichen; Countess Victoria Gleichen: Princess Helena Victoria of Schleswig-Holstein.

The Library at Clonalis, County Roscommon, seat of the O'Conor
family, senior descendants of the last High Kings of Ireland.
On display are O'Carolan's Harp and other relics of Gaelic
Ireland, evoking the spirit of the 'Land of Saints and
Scholars'.

The Marble Hall at Kedleston, Derbyshire, Robert Adam's
masterpiece. The house and contents were rescued by the National
Heritage Memorial Fund and given to the National Trust in 1986.
It remains the family home of the Curzons, Viscounts Scarsdale.

An eighteenth-century conversation piece of one of the great
British families of achievement, the Wedgwoods of Etruria
Hall, Staffordshire.

Glenconner is a great-grandson of Sir Charles Tennant and best known as the proprietor of Mustique in the Caribbean and a friend of its most publicized visitor, Princess Margaret.

The majority of the existing 'Scottish' peerages created during the past hundred years were conferred on prominent business families. Shipping is represented by the Earls of Inchcape and Lord Inverforth; distilling by Lord Forteviot; engineering by Viscount Weir. But many of these peerages were in fact given for reasons other than success in commerce or industry. The 1st Viscount Younger of Leckie, of the brewing family, was Chairman of the Unionist party (the present heir is Secretary of State for Defence); the 1st Viscount Weir and the 1st Lord Inverforth were both members of the government; the 1st Earl of Inchcape was a member of the Council of India. The 1st Lord Clydesmuir also obtained his peerage as a politician and former Governor of Bombay.

Outside the peerage, an example of a fairly recent commercial dynasty are the cotton-rich Stewart-Clark Baronets, who bought the seat of the senior branch of the Dundas family, Dundas Castle overlooking the Forth, towards the end of the nineteenth century. The family cotton-thread works in the town of Paisley near Glasgow became the largest in Britain—if not in the world—after being amalgamated with the works of the other great Paisley thread tycoons, the Coats family. From another branch of the Paisley House of Clark descended the late Lord Clark of *Civilization* fame, whose own family seat is now Saltwood Castle in Kent.

In a special 'semi-royal' category among great Scottish families comes that of the Duke of Fife, who can be listed under the heading 'other members of the royal family'. He is the only great-grandson of King Edward VII residing in the United Kingdom—now at Elsick House in Kincardineshire—being descended from that portly monarch's daughter, Princess Louise, the Princess Royal and Duchess of Fife, who died in 1931. The Dukedom was conferred on Princess Louise's husband, Alexander Duff, 6th Earl of Fife, by Queen Victoria.

It was, of course, Victoria and Albert's purchase of Balmoral in Aberdeenshire that put the Highlands firmly back on the map. Tartan came back into vogue—a chorus of chameleons would have died of over-exertion at Balmoral as 'tartanitis' captured Albert's imagination. The English 'discovery' of the Highlands had really dated from the Romantic Movement and the novels of Sir Walter Scott; it was to be furthered later in the nineteenth century by the British aristocracy's love of sport and by the coming of the railways. The annual northward migration of fashionable aristocratic families to Highland lodges in pursuit of the grouse and the stag still continues today, though to a lesser extent than fifty years ago.

CHAPTER VIII

SOUTH AND NORTH

IRELAND

NO COUNTRY is made up of one stock. The society of any nation usually comprises the indigenous population and a collection of immigrants who have steadily established themselves. Hardly anywhere is the mixture so apparent as it is in Ireland; but, of course, the blending of the different stocks has always been the country's greatest problem as the invasions have come in a series of shock-waves. To the ancient Celtic inhabitants were added repeated surges of settlers.

The effects of the twelfth- and thirteenth-century Anglo-Norman invasions were not, in fact, very great. Even though Henry III was nominally styled *Dominus Hiberniae* from 1259, English authority had still not extended very far by the end of the medieval period. Some of the descendants of the Norman invaders became 'more Irish than the Irish', intermarrying with Celtic families and even forming 'septs' (clans) along Irish lines. Others, particularly, in the 'Pale' (around Dublin) and the south-east, remained distinct from the indigenous Irish dynasties. Together with certain families of Danish origin and the descendants of English who settled in Ireland during the later Middle Ages, they were known as the 'Old English'.

Following the rebellion of 'Silken Thomas' Earl of Kildare, Henry VIII (styled 'King of Ireland' from 1542) began the policy of plantation, establishing English settlers on a significant scale. This policy was accelerated by Mary Tudor on account of the O'More rising and, above all, by Elizabeth in the Settlement of Munster following the great Desmond Rebellions of 1569. In Ulster there was a 'plantation' of Lowland Scots in the wake of the Flight of the Earls (when Hugh O'Neill and the other great Northern Chief, O'Donnell, departed for the Continent) in 1607. Thus a 'British' aristocracy was established with the parcelling out among the settlers of land confiscated during the various rebellions.

Two Prime Ministers with Ulster roots: Sir Alec Douglas-Home (a descendant of the Hamiltons, Dukes of Abercorn) and Captain Terence O'Neill, the Prime Minister of Northern Ireland whose liberal policies upset the lunatic Orange fringe, with disastrous consequences. Now they are life peers as Lord Home of the Hirsel and Lord O'Neill of the Maine respectively.

Shane's Castle, County Antrim, as it was in 1780. The Castle took its name from Shane McBrian O'Neill, a scion of the ancient Irish Royal House who was allowed to keep 120,000 acres of his lands after the early seventeenth-century Plantation of Ulster. It was burnt (traditionally by the disgruntled family banshee) in 1816, rebuilt in the 1860s and burnt again in 1922. The present Lord O'Neill lives in a modern Classical house nearby.

After the Plantation of Ulster the next main influx of the seventeenth century came hard upon the English Civil War Parliamentary victory in the form of a settlement of Cromwellian supporters. The final large settlement by force occurred following William III's defeat of James II in the Williamite Wars. Periodic peaceful settlements from England, Scotland and other European countries were to take place during the eighteenth and nineteenth centuries down to the present day.

There are now about half a dozen or so peers of undoubted Celtic-Irish descent in the male line, accounting for less than a tenth of what can be called 'Irish peers'. Their total comes to more than a hundred if one includes all hereditary peers of Irish or Anglo-Irish stock who still live in Ireland, or whose forebears lived there for an appreciable time after being raised to the peerage — regardless of whether they are 'peers of Ireland' in the strict sense, or peers of the United Kingdom. The question is, of course, complicated by the fact that peerages of Ireland came to be dished out to families who had no connection with Ireland at all, in order to keep their recipients out of the House of Lords at Westminster. Apart from the small Celtic-Irish representation, the rest of the total number of Irish peers can, broadly speaking, be divided into those of 'Old English' stock; those descended from sixteenth- and seventeenth-century settlers; and those of Scottish blood.

Lord Inchiquin is Chief of the O'Briens, one of the great Celtic-Irish families like the O'Neills who produced High Kings of Ireland up until the early Middle Ages. The Inchiquin Barony was conferred by Henry VIII on Morrogh O'Brien, who, having succeeded his elder brother, Conor, as King of Thomond (the present County Clare), did homage to the English Crown. As well as being made a peer, Morrogh O'Brien was allowed to bear the royal arms of England — which his descendants have borne ever since — and to use the English royal livery.

The senior line of the O'Briens became extinct in 1855 and the Inchiquin Barony passed to a junior branch of the family, the O'Briens of Dromoland who, like the Earls of Inchiquin, had been Protestant throughout the Penal times. This meant that their large estates, part of the original O'Brien territory in County Clare, had remained intact. In the Cromwellian period, when they were still Catholic, these lands would almost certainly have been confiscated but for the shrewdness of Maire Ruadh, whose O'Brien husband was killed fighting against the troops of the Regicide, Edmund Ludlow. This formidable woman then offered to marry any Cromwellian officer of Ludlow's choosing; her offer was taken up and she duly married an English cornet of horse — thereby saving the family estates for her O'Brien son. According to one tradition, she wasted no time in dispatching her English husband with a well-aimed kick.

Although, unlike numerous other old Irish potentates, the Lords Inchiquin were not celebrated for rebelling against English rule, it would be wrong to give the impression that they were mere cats'-paws. For instance, as late as 1848 William Smith O'Brien, whose brother inherited the Inchiquin Barony, led an abortive rising. It was suggested that his great-great-nephew, the late Lord Inchiquin, might have become 'Prince-President' of Ireland or even King of a restored Irish monarchy; though he himself showed no inclination to play the role of pretender. The present Lord Inchiquin, who succeeded his brother in 1968, is a geologist by profession and lives in England.

The senior-male-line representative of the O'Neill High Kings is not in fact a peer of the British Crown, but a Portuguese nobleman, The O'Neill of Clannaboy. His kinsman, the present Lord O'Neill, is descended from this great Irish dynasty through a female line. The O'Neills, the most famous branch of the ancient Royal House of Tara, are now, as Sir Iain Moncreiffe of that Ilk pointed out, the oldest traceable family in Europe, with an accepted pedigree dating from the father of Niall 'of the Nine Hostages', King of Ireland in the early years of the fifth century. After ceasing to be Kings of all Ireland, the O'Neills were Kings of Ulster and remained virtual sovereigns until the defeat of Hugh O'Neill, Earl of Tyrone, who led the Irish in a war against the English at the end of Elizabeth I's reign,

A few years later, in 1607, the 'last and one of the greatest of Gaelic kings' went into exile in the Flight of the Earls and most of the vast territories of the O'Neills in Ulster were parcelled out among English and, primarily, Scots settlers. However, one scion of the ancient Royal House, Shane MacBriain O'Neill (described as 'a modest man that speaketh English') was allowed to keep 120,000 acres in County Antrim, together with his castle on Lough Neagh, which subsequently came to be known as Shane's Castle.

This branch of the O'Neills became Viscounts, but the peerage became extinct in 1855. The Shane's Castle estate then passed to the great-grandson of an O'Neill heiress, who changed his name from Chichester to O'Neill and was afterwards raised to the peerage. This 1st Lord O'Neill (of the recent creation), an accomplished musician, built the Victorian Shane's Castle, the original castle having been burnt in 1816 — allegedly by the family banshee, whose nose had been put out of joint by having its room invaded during a particularly large house party. The Victorian castle was itself burnt in 1922 during the 'Troubles' and has now been replaced by a modern house in the Georgian style, which the present Lord O'Neill built a few years ago.

Lord O'Neill, who formerly had the thankless job of chairing the Northern Ireland Tourist Board, has made a tourist attraction at Shane's Castle in the form of a narrow-gauge railway. His father was killed in action in Italy in the last war and his mother, the former Ann Charteris, a prominent hostess, subsequently married first the 2nd Viscount Rothermere and then Ian Fleming, the creator of James Bond. Bamber Gascoigne, the author and television quiz-master, is a first cousin of Lord O'Neill.

The most distinguished modern member of the family is Lord O'Neill's uncle, the statesman, Terence O'Neill, under whose dynamic leadership Northern Ireland came so near to avoiding the onset of the present Troubles. Lord O'Neill of the Maine, as he became when he was made a life peer, is himself the nephew of another O'Neill politician, the late Lord Rathcavan, who was raised to the peerage in 1953.

Of the Celtic-Irish families outside the peerage, the most historic are those descended from ancient kings or chiefs. As one impoverished old chieftain put it: 'My ancestors wore a crown and I haven't got half-a-crown'. The head of the O'Conors of Clonalis, in County Roscommon, is styled O'Conor Don and has the special distinction of being the present senior representative of the High Kings. The O'Conors were indeed the last High Kings of Ireland, Rory O'Conor being High King at the time of the Norman invasion and obliged to acknowledge the supremacy of Henry II. After that they continued to be Kings of Connaught, over which province their dynasty had reigned since the fifth century; and it was not until the time of Elizabeth I that they finally lost their sovereign power.

In Elizabethan times, the son of the last reigning O'Conor Don was transformed, so to speak, by the English into a county magnate, being confirmed in his estates, knighted and returned as a member of parliament. During the century that followed, the lands of the O'Conors dwindled owing to forfeiture and the disabilities which they had suffered through remaining Catholic, though the senior branch of the family managed to keep the estate of Clonalis which is still the family seat.

In the nineteenth century the family fortunes improved: four successive holders of the O'Conor Don title were prominent in public life as members of parliament, Privy Councillors and Lieutenants of the County. The O'Conor Don of the time carried the Standard of Ireland at the Coronation of George V.

Other Celtic-Irish chieftainly families outside the peerage include the MacGillycuddys of the Reeks; the MacDermots, Princes of Coolavin; the O'Donovans; the O'Morchoes and the O'Donoghues of the Glens. 'The Fox' appears to have gone to ground in Australia.

Various other chiefs are represented in the female line, such as The MacMorrough by Andrew MacMorrough Kavanagh of Borris, County Carlow. Borris featured in the saga of the 'Ladies of Llangollen' when Eleanor Butler (whose sister was married to the Chieftain) was kept there in disgrace after she and Sarah Ponsonby had tried to run away together. One of the most remarkable of all Irish Chieftains, Arthur MacMorrough Kavanagh, was born in 1831 without arms or legs, but led an active and adventurous life, rode, shot and travelled in remote parts of Africa and elsewhere, as well as becoming a member of parliament and a Privy Councillor. On one of his visits to Abbey Leix, he remarked to his hostess Lady De Vesci: 'It's an

'The Fair Geraldine': Lady Elizabeth FitzGerald, halfsister
of the 10th Earl of Kildare ('Silken Thomas'). The sixteenth-
century poet Lord Surrey addressed his sonnets to this
Irish beauty.

extraordinary thing—I haven't been here for five years but the station-master recognized me.'

About a quarter of the Irish peers are of 'Old English' descent—the great majority in the male line; a few are from the female line through heiresses. First among the Old English are those two great Anglo-Norman Houses, the FitzGeralds or Geraldines and their traditional rivals, the Butlers, descended from two powerful nobles who came to Ireland in Henry II's invasion. Since the eighteenth century, the FitzGeralds have held the Dukedom of Leinster, the premier peerage of Ireland.

The patriarch of the Geraldines was Maurice FitzGerald, the companion in arms of Strongbow, with whom he captured Dublin in 1170. His descendants were Barons of Offaly from about 1200 and Earls of Kildare from 1316. The 1st Baron took part in the conquest of Limerick and obtained the castle of Croom in that county from which the FitzGeralds took their war cry 'Crom a boo', meaning 'Croom to victory'.

These stirring words now comprise the family motto. The origin of the heraldic monkey in the FitzGerald coat of arms goes back to the legend concerning the early infancy of the 1st Earl of Kildare. The story goes that he was in the castle of Woodstock near Athy when an alarm of fire was raised; in the confusion that ensued, the child was forgotten and when the servants returned to search for him, the room in which he lay was found in ruins. Soon afterwards a strange sound was heard from one of the towers, and on looking up they saw an ape, which was usually kept chained, carefully holding the child in his arms. In gratitude for this act of simian Samaritanism, the Earl afterwards adopted a monkey for his crest.

In the fifteenth and sixteenth centuries the Kildare FitzGeralds reached their apogee as the 'good' family of Ireland. The 8th Earl of Kildare, known as the 'Great Earl' or Garret More, ruled Ireland in the King's name during the latter part of the fifteenth century and the opening years of the sixteenth. He owed his power not to English arms but to his own strength, statesmanship and prestige. The 9th Earl, Garret Óge was in many ways as great a man as his father; but he incurred the hatred of Wolsey and died a prisoner in the Tower of London. Before Garret Óge's death, his son, 'Silken Thomas', who became the 10th Earl, went into rebellion. Having held out against the English for some time, he was obliged to surrender on a promise of pardon which Henry VIII violated. Consequently he and five of his uncles were hanged, drawn and quartered for high treason.

For the remaining years of Henry's reign, the Kildare FitzGeralds were under attainder. It was during this period of disgrace that Silken Thomas's halfsister, Elizabeth, won immortality as 'The Fair Geraldine' to whom the Howard poet, the Earl of Surrey, addressed his sonnets. Meanwhile Silken Thomas's halfbrother and heir wandered about the Continent, acquiring whilst in Florence an interest in alchemy which caused him to be known

The rebellious Lord Edward FitzGerald, leader of the
'Society of United Irishmen' in the 1798 'Year of Liberty'.

(like the Earl of Northumberland a generation later) as the 'Wizard Earl'. He was eventually given back his estates by Edward VI and his titles by Mary.

The principal seat of the Kildare FitzGeralds was Maynooth Castle, but in 1739 the 19th Earl decided to establish himself at Carton nearby and employed the architect Richard Castle to enlarge the house there. The work was completed for his son, the 20th Earl, who became the 1st Duke of Leinster. Together with his beautiful Lennox wife, Emily, he was largely responsible for the great landscaped park. Capability Brown had been consulted, but had said he was too busy to come to Ireland.

A younger son of the 1st Duke, the Republican Lord Edward FitzGerald, was prominent in the 1798 rebellion as a leader of the 'Society of United Irishmen'. Like Silken Thomas, the diminutive Lord Edward was attainted for high treason, but died of wounds received while resisting arrest. Subsequent members of this illustrious Irish dynasty have not played a major part in history. The notorious courtesan Harriette Wilson found the 3rd Duke to be 'a very stingy, stupid blockhead'. When she was living at Kilkea Castle in the 1880s, the attractive wife of the future 5th Duke lamented that 'Kilkea Castle and Lord Kildare/Are more than any woman can bear'.

The Leinsters came into the limelight again this century on account of the vicissitudes of the 7th Duke. This erratic figure signed away his expectations to the 'Fifty Shilling Tailor', Sir Harry Mallaby-Deeley, in return for ready money and annuity, before inheriting the Dukedom from his invalid brother in 1922. As a result of this unhappy transaction he went bankrupt and was in financial difficulties for the rest of his life, finally committing suicide in 1976 at the age of eighty-four.

The present Duke of Leinster, the 7th Duke's son by the first of his four marriages, now lives in Oxfordshire, where he built up a flourishing flying school. Carton was sold in 1949 and the medieval Kilkea, where the present Duke used to live, has now become an hotel.

After the death of the late Duke of Leinster, a Californian claimant to the title emerged, with the unlikely contention that his father, who went under the name of Maurice FitzGerald, had been the 6th Duke. The story went that the 6th Duke of Leinster had not, after all, died in a Scottish asylum, but had emigrated to the United States. Though the yarn received plenty of publicity — as is the way with such melodramatic 'impostor' cases — it carried scant conviction.

The two branches of the House of Geraldine which hold the hereditary Knighthoods of Glin and Kerry descend not from an actual peer, but from the thirteenth-century ancestor of the attainted Earl of Desmond, John FitzThomas. One of the FitzThomas's four illegitimate sons established his authority over West Limerick and was the ancestor of the Knights of Glin; another was the ancestor of the Knights of Kerry. During the reign of Elizabeth I, both families rebelled more than once in support of their kinsmen, the Earls of Desmond. On each occasion they were pardoned and some of their lands restored to them; though Thomas FitzJohn, Knight of Glin, only escaped execution through a legal technicality; and his son and heir was hanged, drawn and quartered.

When the subsequent Knight of Glin, Edmund FitzThomas, was in rebellion, the English beseiged and captured the castle of Glin on the Shannon estuary. During the siege, the castle was bravely defended by a garrison that is said to have included no less than two dozen of the Knight's bastards. Glin was captured again by the English in 1642; and under the Cromwellian Settlement, which followed ten years later, the then Knight was to be transplanted to Connaught. But he stayed in the vicinity of Glin and his nephew and eventual successor recovered the ancestral estate after the Restoration. The Knights of Kerry also managed to survive the seventeenth-century upheavals.

In the eighteenth century, both families conformed to Protestantism and were assimilated into the 'ascendancy'. Robert, Knight of Kerry, was a judge and a member of parliament; the next Knight was also a member of parliament and became a Privy Councillor and a member of the British government. The Knights of Glin were slower than their kinsmen in becoming Anglicized, and kept many of the attributes of old-time Irish potentates until comparatively recently.

The wife of an eighteenth-century Knight of Glin carried out cattle raids in order to obtain meat for the starving people during a famine; she was known locally as the 'bean-tigheama' (the 'female chieftain') and spoke Irish as her natural tongue. Her son, Richard, Knight of Glin, known as 'The Duellist' would shout, whenever he entered a public assembly, 'Is there a Moriarty present?', because of the long-standing feud between the FitzGeralds and the Moriartys—who had taken part in the murder of one of the Earls of Desmond. The nineteenth-century 'Knight of the Women'—so called for obvious reasons—continued the feud, fighting a Protestant clergyman because he was a Moriarty. This lecherous Knight's mother was English, and provided some money which was badly needed to save the family from the consequences of many years of reckless extravagance and to complete the building of the present elegant late-Georgian Glin Castle. Then came 'The Cracked Knight' (the nickname derived from his erratic temperament, the result of concussion in a riding accident), who helped a Fenian to escape and publicly horse-whipped the father of Lord Kitchener for evicting some of his tenants whose ancestors had been followers of the Knights of Glin.

The Knights of Kerry, who since 1880 have also been Baronets, became rather English orientated after Sir Maurice FitzGerald, Knight of Kerry, married a daughter of the international financier, Louis Bischoffsheim. The family acquired estates and country houses in England, and eventually sold their ancestral seat on Valencia Island, just off the Kerry coast—though

Adrian FitzGerald, the only son of the present Knight, now owns a small house on Valencia.

The Knights of Glin and Kerry were among those of the Old English who were once 'more Irish than the Irish', like other branches of the Geraldines and Butlers. The Butlers obtained the Earldom of Ormonde in 1328, a dozen years after the creation of the FitzGerald Earldom of Kildare. From their castle of Kilkenny the Butlers ruled over what was more like a kingdom than an estate — indeed they actually held palatine rights over the neighbouring county of Tipperary. Unlike the Geraldines, however, the Ormonde Butlers were consistently loyal to the English Crown; at many periods from the fourteenth century to the seventeenth they carried on the King's government in Ireland, as Lord-Lieutenant, Lord Deputy or Lord Justice.

The 12th Earl, who rose to being Duke of Ormonde in both the peerage of Ireland and that of England, is known to history as the 'Great Duke of Ormonde'. One of the noblest of Cavaliers, the Great Duke proved himself to be an outstanding statesman as well as a soldier in the Civil War. Under his peacetime government after the Restoration, Ireland was more prosperous than at any other period in the seventeenth century.

The Irish Dukedom of Ormonde became extinct in 1758; but in 1791 a distant cousin, John Butler (brother of Eleanor, one of the Ladies of Llangollen) succeeded in establishing his right to the ancient Earldom, having already inherited Kilkenny Castle and the Ormonde estates. The family was advanced to a Marquessate in the next generation. Kilkenny Castle was lived in by the Ormondes until 1935, after which it stood empty for many years; but in 1967 it was presented by the family to the Irish nation and is now being restored by Office of Works. The present octogenarian Marquess of Ormonde divides his time between a small house in Kilkenny and the United States, where he has spent most of his life.

There is no heir to the Marquessate of Ormonde, and the Earldom may well become dormant, for the succession to it has yet to be established. The most likely heir is Viscount Mountgarret (the descendant of a younger son of a sixteenth-century Earl of Ormonde), a leading figure in the Irish Peers Association which has been campaigning for the right of those who only hold peerages in Ireland to be represented once more in the House of Lords at Westminster.

Another great Anglo-Norman family, the de la Poers, or Powers, settled in County Waterford and their turbulent early history certainly qualifies them for being 'more Irish than the Irish'. By the time of Henry VIII, however, the head of one branch of the Powers was sufficiently Anglicized and law abiding to be made a peer. In the seventeenth century his descendants rose to being Earls of Tyrone.

This Earldom of Tyrone became extinct on the death of the 3rd Earl, whose daughter and heiress, Lady Catherine Power, married a Baronet of

James Butler, 1st 'Great Duke' of Ormonde, Lord-
Lieutenant of Ireland, described John Evelyn as
'a sincere friend, a brave soldier, a virtuous courtier,
a loyal subject, an honest man, a bountiful master and
a good Christian'.

English settler stock, Sir Marcus Beresford, a match said to have been prophesied to Sir Marcus's mother by a ghost of the 2nd Earl of Tyrone. Sir Marcus had a new Earldom of Tyrone conferred on him and his son was made Marquess of Waterford in 1789.

By this time the Beresfords had become the most powerful family in Ireland, occupying the position held by the Geraldines and Butlers in earlier periods. Not only was the 1st Marquess of Waterford a very rich and influential territorial magnate, but his brother, John Beresford, was one of a political triumvirate who ruled Ireland in the decade before the Act of Union with Britain in 1800.

The Beresfords also dominated the contemporary established Church. Another brother of the 1st Marquess was Archbishop of Tuam and was made Lord Decies, thus founding a second Beresford dynasty in the peerage; while the 1st Marquess's second son, Lord John George Beresford, later became Archbishop of Armagh and Primate of All Ireland. This last-mentioned ecclesiastical *grand seigneur*, celebrated for driving up the steep hill to his cathedral in a coach and six, was succeeded at Armagh by yet another Beresford Archbishop. It was popularly considered that if the family attained the Primacy a third time running they should have it for keeps, like a racing cup. As well as having brothers and a son who were powerful in Church and state, the 1st Marquess of Waterford had a famous illegitimate son, the mighty Marshal Beresford, who reorganized the Portuguese army during the Peninsular War and helped to rule Portugal when the King was absent in Brazil.

The notion of a racing cup for the Episcopacy is certainly an appropriate analogy for the family as the Beresfords became a byword for horsemanship. The 3rd Marquess was one of the great hunting men of his time and Ralph Nevill has given us a glimpse of some of his eccentricities in *Sporting Days and Sporting Ways*:

> He painted the Melton toll-bar a bright red, put aniseed on the hoofs of a parson's horse and hunted the terrified divine with bloodhounds. On another occasion he put a donkey into the bed of a stranger at an inn . . . and solemnly proposed to one of the first railway companies in Ireland to start two engines in opposite directions on the same line in order that he might witness the smash, for which he proposed to pay.

The sporting exploits of the three brothers of the 5th Marquess (who shot himself after suffering for many years from a bad fall in the hunting field) were legendary. The brothers were Lord Charles Beresford ('Charlie B'), the adventurous admiral, who had a hunt in full cry tattooed down his back with the fox going to earth in the appropriate aperture; Lord William Beresford, who won the VC in the Zulu War; and Lord Marcus Beresford, who managed the racing stables of Edward IV and George V. The present Marquess of

In 1904 King Edward VII and Queen Alexandra stayed with
the Marquess and Marchioness of Ormonde at Kilkenny Castle
(where baths were specially installed for the first time).
This is an artist's impression of the great reception
held for Their Majesties in the picture gallery of the
Castle.

Pakenham Hall, County Westmeath, seat of the Pakenhams and
one of the first houses in the British Isles to be centrally
heated. The present owner, Thomas Pakenham, the historian
heir of the Earl of Longford, has restored the Castle's
original Irish name of Tullynally by which it is now known.

Waterford and his brother Lord Patrick Beresford have carried on the sporting traditions of the family, particularly as polo players. Their first cousin is the architectural historian, Mark Girouard. Lord Waterford still lives at Curraghmore, the family seat in County Waterford, where the old castle of the Powers now forms part of a mainly Georgian mansion, in the midst of the most magnificent demesne in Ireland.

Curraghmore is one of the very few major Irish country houses still lived in by their original families and maintained in something like the style of former times. Another is Dunsany Castle in County Meath, a castle with a medieval exterior and an interior that is elegantly Georgian. This is the seat of the Plunketts, Lords Dunsany. The present Lord Dunsany's father was a noted poet and dramatist and his great-uncle was Sir Horace Plunkett, the Irish agricultural reformer. Although the Plunketts were probably in Ireland before the Norman invasion, being of Danish origin, they belong very much to the Old English group and are typical of the medieval aristocracy of the Pale, having constantly intermarried with families of Anglo-Norman stock. The other Plunkett peer, the Earl of Fingall, is one of the few present-day Irish peers with an unbroken Catholic tradition in his family.

Many of the great Anglo-Norman or Old English families in Ireland descended not from feudal lords but from merchants in the towns. Richard Caddell, the progenitor of all the numerous dynasties of Blake was Portreeve (the equivalent of Mayor) of Galway about 1300. This surname is derived from his nickname of 'Niger' or 'Black'. From then until the seventeenth century, the Blakes were prominent among the merchant aristocracy of the town, which eventually consisted of fourteen families known afterwards as the 'Tribes'.

The Blakes produced several landed branches including the Baronets of Menlough. The 12th Baronet, Sir John Blake, is said to have been made a member of parliament to give him immunity from his creditors. According to the story, when he had been duly elected, his constituents came in a body to Menlough and called him ashore from the boat in which he was sitting in order to avoid two process-servers who were waiting for him on the river bank. The head of the Ardfry branch of the Blakes was made Lord Wallscourt in 1800—a title which became extinct in 1920. The 3rd Lord Wallscourt, a man of exceptional strength prone to acts of violence, found it restful to walk about the house naked; his wife persuaded him to carry a cowbell when he was in this state so as to warn the maidservants of his approach.

On the whole, the Englishmen who acquired estates in Ireland under the Tudors came from the landed aristocracy: they were either younger sons, or heads of families which had become impoverished. The same was true of the Scots who were granted land in Ulster in the reign of James I. Of the peers of English settler stock—who make up half the total of Irish peers—the most historically important, the descendants of Richard Boyle, the Great Earl of

Cork, have long since passed from the Irish scene. Boyle, who came from a family of some standing in Kent, for all his initial shortage of cash was able to buy 42,000 acres in Cork and Waterford at a knock-down price from Sir Walter Raleigh, and he established colonies of English on these lands, as well as building towns and starting industries. Among the several peers who were pleased to marry the daughters of the great settler Earl were two of Norman-Irish descent but of the Protestant religion: the Earl of Kildare, head of the Leinster FitzGeralds, and the Earl of Barrymore, head of the Barrys.

The Moores, Earls of Drogheda, and Binghams, Earls of Lucan, are two further examples of Elizabethan settler families who are no longer in Ireland. Where the present Earl of Lucan has been since the murder of his children's nanny in 1974 remains an open question. But the Earl of Drogheda is very much in the centre of English life as a Knight of the Garter and friend of the royal family, and has been responsible for running both the *Financial Times* and the Royal Opera House, Covent Garden. His son, Viscount Moore, one of the ever-increasing number of aristocrats who have taken up photography as a career, is best known for his books on American architecture.

Irish peerage families of Cromwellian stock are not nearly so numerous as is sometimes assumed. Only a dozen or so can be counted in this category, including the Pakenhams, Earls of Longford, and Ponsonbys, Earls of Bessborough. Although, again, both these Earls now live in England, the heir to the Earldom of Longford, Thomas Pakenham, still lives at Tullynally, the family seat in County Westmeath, and a fine example of early nineteenth-century Gothic-revival architecture. Mr Pakenham (who does not use a courtesy title) is the author of books on the Irish rebellion of 1798 and the Boer War. It is, of course, in the world of books rather than that of the martial arts that the Pakenhams are now famous. This prolific literary family, headed by Lord Longford himself and his wife Elizabeth, also includes their daughters Lady Antonia Fraser (now married to Harold Pinter) and Lady Rachel Billington, as well as Lord Longford's sisters, Lady Violet Powell (wife of the great novelist Anthony Powell) and Lady Mary Clive.

Moving north to Ulster, one finds that by no means all the Ulster peers are of Scottish descent. In fact one can find as many English surnames as Scottish among Northern Irish families in the peerage. Viscount Brookeborough is a case in point from among the English settler group. His family estate in County Fermanagh, adjoining the town of Brookeborough, was granted in the seventeenth century to his ancestor, Sir Henry Brooke, who fought for parliament during the Civil War. Sir Henry's father, Sir Basil Brooke, was an English soldier who served in Ireland under Eizabeth I and obtained large territorial grants in County Donegal.

As landowners in the magnate class, the Brookes might well have risen to the peerage during the eighteenth century or early in the nineteenth; instead, they obtained nothing more than a Baronetcy. The grandfather of the present Lord Brookeborough, who received a Viscountcy in 1952, was Sir Basil Brooke, 5th Baronet. He held the office of Prime Minister of Northern Ireland from 1943 to 1963 — a spell that recalled that of Walpole, at least in his tendency to let sleeping dogs lie. The late Viscount was also a Northern Ireland Cabinet minister. The present Viscount has recently moved back into the imposing seat of Colebrooke, whose dining-room encrusted with deer skulls was christened 'Golgotha' by Lord Craigavon, the first Prime Minister of Northern Ireland.

The Brooke family also produced the brilliant Field Marshal Viscount Alanbrooke who was appointed Chief of the Imperial General staff during the Second World War. By a remarkable coincidence, Alanbrooke was one of six contemporary Field Marshals who all came from Ulster. The others were Alexander (brother of the 5th Earl of Caledon), Auchinleck, Dill, Montgomery and Montgomery-Massingberd.

Naturally the majority of the twenty-odd Irish peers of Scottish descent are — or have been — connected with Ulster. They include the Hamiltons, Dukes of Abercorn, and the Vane-Tempest-Stewarts, Marquesses of Londonderry. The latter were as influential in Ulster as the former until a generation or so ago, but the present Lord Londonderry lives entirely in England and the family seat of Mount Stewart is now looked after by the National Trust.

The Irish patriarch of the Abercorn Hamiltons was unlike the other Lowland Scots settlers in already being a peer and a very grand one at that. This 1st Earl of Abercorn, a royal favourite who obtained the family estates in County Tyrone, was a grandson of James Hamilton, Earl of Arran — no less a personage than the heir presumptive to the Scottish throne and Regent of Scotland during the minority of Mary Stuart.

The 2nd Earl of Abercorn, who actually became head of the House of Hamilton when his cousin, the 2nd Duke of Hamilton, died leaving no son, was a Catholic like his mother. The 4th Earl differed from most of the Ulster-Scots aristocracy by fighting for King James in the Williamite War and was consequently outlawed. However, the family did not suffer on account of the 4th Earl's Jacobitism as the eventual heir was a Protestant who had gone over to the side of William III.

At the end of the eighteenth century, the 9th Earl was made Marquess of Abercorn. He was known as 'Don Magnifico' and celebrated for 'Castilian pomp', pride and eccentricity, as well as for his fabulous entertainments at Bentley Priory near Stanmore in Middlesex. GE Russell recorded in his *Collections and Recollections* that:

> He is stated to have always gone out shooting in his Blue Ribbon, and to have required his housemaids to wear white kid gloves when they made his bed. It is also alleged that having learnt of this second wife's contemplated elopement, he sent her a message begging her to take the

The wedding of Frank Pakenham and Elizabeth Harman, a surgeon's daughter, at St Margaret's Westminster in 1931. Now the Earl and Countess of Longford, they preside over Britain's best-known literary dynasty.

Louisa Duchess of Abercorn photographed with over 100 of her descendants in July 1894. As all her seven daughters married high-ranking peers, the Abercorn cousinhood now embraces almost everybody one can think of within the great British families including such royal brides as the Princess of Wales and the Duchess of York.

family coach, as it ought never to be said that Lady Abercorn left her husband's roof in a hack chaise.

Don Magnifico's grandson, who was twice Lord-Lieutenant of Ireland, was made Duke of Abercorn in 1868 on the recommendation of Disraeli, who claimed that by thus elevating him, he had actually increased his physical stature.

The 1st Duke of Abercorn and his redoubtable Duchess, who was herself the daughter of a Duke of Bedford, had seven daughters — each of whom married either a duke, a marquess or an earl. Thus an astonishing number of families in the higher ranks of the present-day peerage are descended from them: this is a prime key to the labyrinthine network of great British families. Before she died in 1905 Duchess Louisa had over 160 living descendants and there was a famous photograph taken with 101 of them in July 1894. There is also a photograph of her with her first great-great-grandson, the infant Alec Douglas-Home, who was destined to become Prime Minister of Great Britain in succession to Harold Macmillan whose wife was her great-granddaughter.

The present Princess of Wales is also a descendant of the Abercorns. Her paternal grandmother, the late Countess Spencer, a Lady of the Bedchamber to the Queen Mother, was a sister of the 4th Duke, whose widow is the Queen Mother's Mistress of the Robes. The present Duke's sister, Lady Moyra Campbell, was a lady-in-waiting to Princess Alexandra for many years.

The Dukes of Abercorn are very much the first family of Northern Ireland; the 3rd Duke became its first Governor in 1922 and held the office until 1945. The present Duke also made a name for himself in public life by representing Fermanagh and South Tyrone in the House of Commons before he succeeded to the Dukedom. Since the Dukedom of Abercorn is in the peerage of Ireland, whereas the Marquessate and Earldom of Abercorn are in the peerages of Great Britain and Scotland respectively, the Duke of Abercorn has the distinction of holding titles in the peerages of all three kingdoms. For full measure, he also holds the French Dukedom of Chatellerault, which Henri II conferred on the Duke's sixteenth ancestor, the Regent Arran.

When the present Duke (then styled Marquess of Hamilton) had a son in 1969, there was an embarrassing problem over what the boy himself should be styled. Usually the eldest grandson of a Duke of Abercorn is known as Lord Paisley. In view of the modern connotations of that name in Northern Ireland, however, it was thought wiser to opt for the alternative of Viscount Strabane.

With the exception of Belfast, Ireland was not much affected by the Industrial Revolution. None the less, nineteenth-century Irish aristocratic society included a few rich industrialists, who built large country houses for themselves during the fifty years following the Famine when the longer-

One of the famous 'Guinness girls', Maureen, Marchioness
of Dufferin and Ava, arrives for a royal garden party at
Buckingham Palace with her parents, Mr and Mrs Ernest Guinness.

established landed dynasties could mostly no longer afford to build. Among them was the Belfast linen family of Mulholland (who became Lords Dunleath) and, of course, the even richer Dublin brewing family of Guinness. It could be argued that the two Guinness peers, the Earl of Iveagh and Lord Moyne should really belong to the Celtic-Irish group at the beginning of this chapter, for the Guinnesses probably descend from a branch of the ancient sept of Magennis which inhabited the territory of Iveagh in what is now County Down—though there is also a theory that they may be of Cornish origin and that their name was originally Gennys.

The story of the Guinnesses is a fascinating object lesson in Anglo-Irish social history. As merchant princes who make nonsense of the mythical aristocratic 'trade' taboo, they are unsnobbishly proud of their comparatively recent foundation by the banks of the Liffey and remain closely allied to the businesses from which their vast fortunes stem. In Ireland the Guinnesses are virtually regarded as royalty and they also possess an international chic, a patrician panache, that makes them one of the most stylish families in the world. Their remarkable contributions to philanthropy and the arts, and their supply of public figures have shown that they are far more than mere sybarites.

Arthur Guinness and his son and namesake established the Dublin brewery in the late eighteenth and early nineteenth centuries; the grandson developed the brewery, became Lord Mayor of Dublin, restored the Cathedral and was made a Baronet. Two of the latter's sons became peers (as the Earl of Iveagh and Lord Ardilaun); two of them married daughters of Earls; and a daughter married another peer who was also Archbishop of Dublin. The philanthropist 1st Earl of Iveagh bought estates in England, establishing a famous shoot at Elvedon in Suffolk where he entertained the fashionable Edwardians—including Albert Edward himself as Prince of Wales and also as King.

The present Earl of Iveagh, unlike his grandfather and predecessor, the agriculturalist 2nd Earl (who was very much English orientated), identifies himself entirely with Ireland, though still owning a large English estate. He has made his home at Farmleigh, a Victorian mansion in a demesne adjoining Dublin's Phoenix Park, which his grandfather used only for occasional visits from Elveden and Ken Wood (the Hampstead treasure-house now run by English Heritage). As well as being chairman of the family firm, the present Lord Iveagh was formerly a member of the Irish Senate; despite being plagued by ill health he plays an active part in Irish life generally and particularly in matters to do with the arts.

The youngest son of the 1st Earl of Iveagh, who became the 1st Lord Moyne, was a prominent politician who played a significant role in the history of the Middle East. After his assassination in 1944 by the Stern Gang when Minister of State in Cairo, he was succeeded by the poet Bryan

Desmond Guinness, the president of the Irish Georgian
Society, and his first wife Princess Marie-Gabrielle
von Urach, who have been such stylish forces in the uphill
struggle of persuading Ireland that she has a heritage
worth preserving.

Guinness, whose first wife was Diana Mitford (later Lady Mosley), of the celebrated sisterhood. The present Lord Moyne divides his time between two country houses, one in Hampshire and the other in Dublin. His elder son, the flamboyant Jonathan Guinness, now concentrates on banking after some well-publicized political forays. The second son, Desmond, the preservationist, architectural writer and founder of the Irish Georgian Society, lives at Leixlip Castle in County Kildare — just near where the founding father, Richard Guinness, had a brewery in the mid-eighteenth century.

Desmond Guinness's first wife Mariga, a striking Württemberg Princess, is one of a galaxy of modern Guinness women. Their number has included the banker Loel Guinness's exotic third wife Gloria and his daughter Lindy, the artist, who is married to the present Marquess of Dufferin and Ava. Lord Dufferin's mother, the redoubtable Maureen, is herself a Guinness by birth; her daughter Caroline Blackwood, the novelist, is the widow of the American poet Robert Lowell, having previously been married to Lucian Freud and Israel Citkowitz. Maureen's sisters are Aileen Lady Plunket and Oonagh Lady Oranmore and Browne, the mother of Gay Kindersley, the jockey, and of the colourful Garech Browne and his brother Tara. The latter was a 1960s' cult figure immortalized in the Beatles' song 'A Day in the Life' following his death in a London car smash. In the present generation the beauties in the family include Sabrina and her twin sister Miranda, not to mention Catherine, reputed to be the only female allowed to accompany Andy Warhol to The Toilet (a *louche* New York nightclub), and now the wife of Lord Neidpath, the flamboyant if scholarly son of the Earl of Wemyss.

The suicide of the present Earl of Iveagh's younger sister — one of a considerable number of Guinness women to have married foreigners — and the tragic death at Oxford of Olivia Channon (another scion of the 'Guinnessty') prompted some people to trace a pattern of tragedy that has stalked the family, as if it amounted to a sort of curse on the House of Guinness. This is naturally absurd, though it may be hard to escape the impression that the family has had more than their actuarial share of misfortune.

The Guinnesses provide a classic example of the traditional progression of a great family from business to money — to titles and land — to activity in the world of the arts. Their adoption of an 'Anglo' persona and subsequent resumption of a commitment to Ireland also epitomizes what has happened to the dwindling Anglo-Irish aristocracy.

CHAPTER IX

AN EMPTY COFFIN?

What between the duties expected of one during one's lifetime, and the duties exacted from one after one's death, land has ceased to be either a profit or a pleasure. It gives one position, and prevents one from keeping it up. That's all that can be said about land.

Lady Bracknell in *The Importance of Being Earnest* (1895)

OSCAR WILDE wrote that famous speech with the authority of an emigrant son of an Irish landlord at a time when land was indeed almost becoming a liability rather than an asset in Britain. The great slump in farming in the 1880s and 1890s ruined many landed families; and, by a melancholy coincidence, it was in 1888 that the land-owners' authority in local government was brought to an end by the setting up of county and rural district councils.

There was another acute agricultural depression in the years between the 1914–18 and 1939–45 wars. Things became so bad that one large landowner actually offered to pay people to come and be tenants on his estate. Land, it was thought, would never recover and many families who had no option but to sell up counted themselves lucky to receive the rock-bottom prices.

Taxation rose sharply after 1918 and continued to rise; matters were not improved by the Stock Market collapse of 1929. The 1920s saw the sale, and often the destruction, of the great town houses; also some important country seats were sold off and demolished, such as Hamilton Palace in Lanarkshire. Of course the magnates who derived income from sources like town property, local mines and harbours, suffered less than those families whose rural acres were their only asset. But a general feeling of decline could be sensed and the outbreak of the Second World War seemed to mark the end of the epoch of great British families.

It was in a mood of passionate nostalgia for this world which had appa-rently vanished that Evelyn Waugh wrote *Brideshead Revisited* in 1944. To

Waugh it seemed that 'the ancestral seats which were our chief national artistic achievement were doomed to decay and spoliation like the monasteries in the sixteenth century'. And yet, when the novelist revised *Brideshead* fifteen years later, he felt bound to admit in the preface that the aristocracy had maintained its identity to a degree that would have seemed impossible towards the end of the war. Much of the book was therefore, in Waugh's words, 'a panegyric preached over an empty coffin'.

What had happened? The answer, of course, lay in the soil. Those who had faith in the future and managed to hang on to their acres, sometimes at considerable sacrifice, began to be rewarded — at least on paper — by the steady rise in value of agricultural land. Thanks to the 1950s' boom, the great British families made a remarkable recovery.

In his preface to the new edition of *Brideshead Revisited*, Evelyn Waugh also commented on the contemporary 'cult of the country house'. As early as 1935 Osbert Sitwell was writing of country houses: 'Alas! how curious it is that these works of art only begin to obtain a wide appreciation when they are on the verge of being destroyed.' By the late 1950s the stately home industry was in full swing and Waugh observed that 'Brideshead today would be open to trippers, its treasures rearranged by expert hands and the fabric better maintained than it was by Lord Marchmain'. But paradoxically the 1950s also witnessed the destruction of more country houses than any other decade this century. In many cases the houses had been requisitioned during the War and were thought to be beyond repair; in others, however 'affluent' life was then meant to be, the families simply could not afford to live in what were considered to have become anachronisms.

The mid-1970s were something of a watershed in the fortunes of the great British families and the magnificent heritage they had created. The memorable exhibition on the 'Destruction of the Country House' at the Victoria and Albert Museum in 1974 created a tremendous impact, serving to remind people how much the aristocracy had achieved in the arts and how fragile were the chances of preserving this heritage in an increasingly unsympathetic economic climate. Apart from the horrors of capital taxation which had been introduced in the Wilson years, inflation rocketed after the 'energy crisis' of 1973. Chancellor Healey's remarks about making the 'pips squeak' created alarm about the future; the prospect of a wealth tax, in addition to capital gains tax and the new capital transfer tax, seemed to hold out little hope for the privately owned heritage.

To counter this threat, the 'heritage lobby' came into existence. In 1973 the owners of country houses banded together to form the Historic Houses Association, which soon established itself as a highly effective organization representing the interests of the private proprietor in the corridors of power. Under its successive presidents, Lord Montagu of Beaulieu, Lord Howard of Henderskelfe (otherwise George Howard of Castle Howard) and Commander

Commander Michael Saunders Watson, the acutely nimble,
engaging and effective president of the Historic Houses
Association (the 'trade union' of the private owner),
outside his family seat of Rockingham Castle, an old
royal fortress in Northamptonshire.

Michael Saunders Watson of Rockingham Castle, the HHA has exerted influence and won results out of all proportion to its years.

Wisely operating on an all-party basis, the HHA fought successfully against the introduction of a wealth tax and helped to educate politicians in the problems faced by those struggling to maintain this unique heritage. Public opinion also seems to have helped the main political parties realize that it is desirable, indeed essential, to create a suitable fiscal, financial and legislative environment for the survival of historic houses, their collections and their parks and gardens.

Among the campaigns the HHA and the heritage lobby have waged is that for an extension of tax relief on repairs and maintenance, which at present benefits only owners of houses which attract large numbers of visitors and are effectively run as businesses. Some relief from capital transfer tax was provided by the 1976 Finance Act but the consequences of the recent introduction of 'inheritance tax' remain to be seen. The HHA and the heritage lobby have also pressed for more helpful provisions on the dreaded value added tax (which is imposed on repairs); and for 'listed' building repair allowances.

All these modern financial technicalities have become of vital importance to the owners of historic houses. A much more hard-headed and professional approach to the whole business of landowning has grown up thanks to the spreading of the word by the HHA and the Country Landowners' Association. The 2,000 or so surviving 'family estates' are now not only worth more than at any other time in their history—even allowing for the plummeting of the pound—but also, as a whole, far more efficiently and profitably run. The agent of a large estate now tends to be a man whose business and administrative skills are such as would qualify him for the managing directorship of a fair-sized commercial empire.

'An historic house without land', says Lord Saye and Sele, the owner of Broughton Castle in Oxfordshire, 'is like a torch without a battery or a mill without a wheel.' As he pointed out, it is the rents the Fiennes family derive from their estate, and the profits from the farming, that enables them to look after the fabric of Broughton and keep it in good condition. In his view, Lady Bracknell's remarks about land in *The Importance of Being Earnest* could be turned on their head.

It is when a house becomes divorced from its land that the problems often arise. This was the case, of course, at Mentmore and at Warwick Castle—those two *causes célèbres* of the 1970s. In 1978 Lord Brooke (as he then was, before succeeding to the Earldom of Warwick) sold Warwick Castle and its remaining contents to Madame Tussaud's—a foretaste, perhaps, of a future when Britain's stately homes are owned by the leisure industry—but before selling the castle itself, he sold some of its treasures piecemeal. This provoked an outcry. 'Many families have battled against hopeless odds, against punitive

The tragic and unnecessary sale at Mentmore (*above*) in
1977 which the Labour Government could easily have
prevented by accepting the Earl of Rosebery's generous
offer. Happily, however, some of the best pieces of
French furniture in the family collection are now on show
at the Roseberys' Scottish seat of Dalmeny (*below*).

taxes and ungrateful governments', Lord Brooke's cousin, Miss Priscilla Greville, wrote sadly to *The Times*. 'They do so because they (and I) are indeed aware of the stature of our forefathers and of our duty to the history that they left us.' On the other hand, some felt that, however regrettable Lord Brooke's actions, what he did with his own property was his own affair. The issue certainly focused attention on how much the 'national heritage' owes to the goodwill of a few great families.

The Mentmore fiasco, when the Labour government failed to take advantage of the Earl of Rosebery's generous offer of the whole caboodle before he dispersed the Rothschild treasures of his grandmother's family, led to the setting up of the National Heritage Memorial Fund as a sort of safety net for heritage property. Under its first Chairman, Lord Charteris of Amisfield, formerly Private Secretary to the Queen, the Fund quickly made its mark by saving that quintessentially English manor house, Canons Ashby in Northamptonshire, the seat of the Drydens—and another place to have become separated from its agricultural estate. After Canons Ashby, the Fund went on to rescue in rapid succession Belton in Lincolnshire (seat of the Custs, Lord Brownlow), Fyvie Castle in Aberdeenshire (the Forbes-Leith Baronets), Calke Abbey in Derbyshire (the reclusive Harpur-Crewes) and the nearby Kedleston (the Curzons, Viscount Scarsdale).

The recipients of all these places, the National Trusts (the National Trust and the National Trust for Scotland), popularly regarded as the longstops for all the problems of the heritage, can in fact now only take on historic houses that are properly endowed. The 'digesting' of a major country house and its estate, and then putting them on show, naturally pose enormous problems for the National Trust which is a charity almost entirely dependent upon the generosity of the public. It seems clear that the Trust's future will lie more in terms of its original object of protecting the countryside than in taking on the running of too many more country houses; it has already embraced about 200 since its country-house scheme started in the late 1930s. Its sister organization north of the border, the National Trust for Scotland (whose president, the Earl of Wemyss is the brother of Lord Charteris of Amisfield), also cares for many historic properties and has made a major contribution to international conservationist policy. Wherever possible, the Trusts try to preserve the houses in their care as the houses of the families associated with them; though, inevitably, this connection cannot always be kept up.

The National Trust is also active in Northern Ireland, but the Republic in the south still has no comparable organization to safeguard the Irish heritage. Until Ireland's entry into the Common Market, the Irish landowners did not benefit to the same degree as landowners in the United Kingdom from improved land values. Until the short-lived Irish economic boom in the 1970s, most of them, in fact, were fairly impoverished. In 1903 the Land Purchase Act (always known as the 'Wyndham Act' after its author, George

Castle Howard, Yorkshire, the location for *Brideshead
Revisited*, the filming of which established a useful
standard commercial contract for houseowners. Posing on
the vintage car are three members of the cast: Anthony
Andrews (a lamentably unconvincing Lord Sebastian Flyte,
with the teddy bear Aloysius); Diana Quick (Lady Julia
Flyte); and Jeremy Irons (Charles Ryder).

Wyndham) had finally settled the vexatious Irish land question by simply stopping the whole concept of a family estate dependent on the rent of tenant farmers. Suddenly the average ownership of land among the landlords was reduced from thousands of acres to the low hundreds. Despite the 'bonus' (as the compensation was known), for many Anglo-Irish dynasties it became an unequal struggle to survive. The plight of the country house too has been worse in the Irish Republic than in Britain, with for three years the ultimate horror of a wealth tax, despite the valiant efforts of such bodies as the Irish Georgian Society which Desmond Guinness started in 1958 to save the elegant eighteenth-century buildings that were being pulled down because of a feeling that they were 'not really Irish'. The 'New Ireland' will persist in seeing these buildings as 'monuments of landlordism and oppression'.

One of the particular problems for the Irish country-house owner is that there is also no equivalent of the Historic Buildings Council to give grants for repairs. In Britain such grants—and most other forms of assistance, like tax relief—are only given on condition that the house in question is opened regularly to the public. This is, in short, why most places are available for the popular gaze, though some owners—and indeed their ancestors—have always enjoyed throwing open their doors to the appreciative visitor. Castle Howard, for instance, has always been open to the public. In 1756, the 4th Earl of Carlisle (whose father began building this sublime palace) built an inn so as to enable tourists to make an early start on the house in the morning. His descendant, the late Lord Howard of Henderskelfe, took a suitably eighteenth-century view: 'I am used to the public', he said. 'Indeed I would feel unhappy if I wasn't sharing Castle Howard with people. Privacy is a nineteenth-century taste. One should remember that park walls were put up to keep the deer in, not the people out.'

The legend of great families making large sums of money by opening their houses to the public is mostly based on a few stately homes like Woburn which have been turned into highly commercialized places of entertainment. For while aristocratic 'showbiz' can pay dividends, it can also lead to disastrous losses. Even when the showbusiness makes a profit, this may not be enough to pay for the upkeep of the home and grounds—particularly as the earned income of stately homes is heavily taxed.

When the net takings from the lions and other tripper attractions of Longleat are set against the cost of the daily maintenance and repair of the splendid Elizabethan house, Lord Bath is left with an ever-increasing annual overdraft—as he himself has pointed out. The Belton saga was an object lesson in the dangers of 'the numbers game'. In a few seasons Lord Brownlow boosted the visiting figures at the late-Stuart showplace from some 20,000 to over 200,000, but somehow Belton never seemed able to contain its costs and to generate enough surplus income in the summer to survive in the winter. 'Big numbers', said the beleaguered Lord Brownlow, 'may mean a substantial turnover, but big numbers are not synonymous with big profits — only continuing losses.'

During the agricultural boom that flourished up to the early 1980s, it almost began to look as if many country-house owners had never had it so good. More and more land was taken 'in hand', so that the owners could farm it profitably themselves. The results were highly gratifying for the maintenance of both the house and the estate.

Indeed the 'doom-gloom' of the heritage lobby even seemed like camouflage hiding a new confidence in the Thatcher era. John Martin Robinson's seminal survey of *The Latest Country Houses* (1984) blew the 'cover' of crisis and decay by revealing to an astounded audience that no less than 200 proper new country houses had been built since the Second World War. 'The subject', wrote Dr Robinson, 'could almost be subtitled "furtive house-building" as the owners have not been particularly keen to draw attention to their enterprise in this field'. Significantly the owners in question turned out to be drawn mainly from the great families such as the Howards, Stanleys, Gordons, Grosvenors, O'Neills, Morrisons and Barings. Moreover, the houses, for the most part substantial neo-Georgian edifices with plenty of servant accommodation, were built on traditional flourishing estates.

Before there was enough time to digest these somewhat awkward facts, a new crisis loomed in the shape of a sudden slide in agricultural profits in the mid-1980s. On the face of it, this seemed to spell disaster for the great families and their power bases. But yet again such a prognostication would be to underestimate the chameleon-like qualities of the country-house owner set upon survival. The species has a shrewd awareness of the need to diversify.

Politically, the heritage has considerably more 'clout' if it can be seen to be serious and worthwhile: conservation is needed rather than circuses, education as well as entertainment. Historic houses stand to benefit more from their use as places in which to learn about the past than as funfairs and certainly in recent years there has been a noted increase in the number of school parties making educational visits. More and more places have organized some form of educational service with the help of the Heritage Education Trust.

Thus, aside from farming, all the other potential sources of income are now being exploited to the full. These range from time-honoured aristocratic pursuits such as forestry and game preservation to the more novel enterprises based on the ever-increasing influx of town-dwellers to the countryside for recreation. In short, 'Leisure Not Wheat' became the new slogan for survival.

And, if opening a country house to the public is hardly ever profitable in itself, the proceeds can still make a useful contribution to the upkeep, while the losses can usually be set off against tax. The money to be made, though, is not in the 'numbers game' but rather in the ancillary activities such as 'functions', conferences and corporate gatherings, film and location work (in the wake of the *Brideshead* breakthrough) and all manner of commercial wheezes. Not so long ago the idea of 'paying guests' in country houses would have been regarded as embarrassingly vulgar; today owners are falling over each other to offer hospitality — so long as the 'punters' are foreign and 'loaded'. Estate buildings are being busily adapted into craft centres, high-technology units, shops, restaurants, hotels, garden centres, 'leisure complexes' and so forth.

Unfortunately not every country-house owner can manage to spread his resources in this way. It is the 'poor relations' whose minor manors and hidden halls are every bit as important to the so-called 'national' heritage (though the 'nation' has, of course, had nothing to do with it) that are the real cause for despair. The sadness is that the lesser aristocracy, which is now fast disappearing, has always been associated with the best gentlemanly values, being less exposed than the magnate class to the corrupting influence of great wealth.

Whatever the misfortunes of the lesser landowners, which represent a different subject, the great families still somehow seem to go from strength to strength even in the face of ostensibly overwhelming odds against them. It is, of course, the survival of the fittest; the race to the swift, the shrewd, and sometimes the downright tough. The will to survive has turned many members of great families into tycoons; contrary to Nancy Mitford's crack that the aristocracy is not very good at making money, the modern age has produced some remarkable aristocratic commercial competitors, frequently in far from traditional spheres. A new entrepreneurial spirit is evident.

Despite all the problems of inheritance, one can predict that a rich hard core will remain. Notwithstanding the paramount importance of landowning in the history of the great families, it is possible that the threat of territorial nationalization may persuade this hard core to go off and live in luxury abroad. And yet, happily, there is plenty of evidence around that *noblesse oblige* still exists in the countryside, with the great families very much continuing to play their part. The urbane Earl of Shelburne, the heir to the Marquess of Lansdowne and regarded as the coming man of the heritage movement in his role as deputy president of the Historic Houses Association, sees the big estates as sheet anchors for housing and employment. At a local meeting in Sussex, the Earl of March, heir to the Duke of Richmond, was told that there was more faith in him bringing about a speed restriction than in the county council doing so. Lord March, whom Lord Shelburne succeeded in the deputy presidency of the HHA, sees the 'big house' as the centre of a local community; there is no doubt that the stately-home industry has brought trade and ancillary opportunities to neighbouring areas. Lord Saye and Sele speaks for many country-house owners when he says: 'We do need help and support, not for ourselves, because no one, least of all the government, owes us anything, but because as trustees, custodians of this

The Earl of Shelburne, owner of the booming Bowood,
Wiltshire, and very much a coming man in the great heritage
movement. He is currently deputy president of the
Historic Houses Association and also an English Heritage commissioner.

Lord Camoys, the City merchant banker, who has fought
gallantly to preserve his ancient family seat of Stonor
in Oxfordshire.

living tradition, I believe we can do the job better, and certainly cheaper, than anyone else.' Lord Brownlow wondered what it is that motivates owners: is it emotion, tax planning for the future, idealism or dynastic considerations? 'I suppose we are all involved in a sort of crusade', he said.

Lord Camoys certainly showed crusading courage in his rescue of the family seat of Stonor in Oxfordshire. No other house in England, it is claimed, not even Windsor Castle, has been so long in continuous occupation by one family; but in 1975 a tragedy seemed about to be enacted. Faced with spiralling taxation and heavy costs, the late Lord Camoys put Stonor on the market. There was a sale in the house and many of the contents were sold. Family problems and taxes made it appear likely that the place would end up in corporate ownership, or be converted into separate units and an antiques centre. Before a purchaser could be found for the house, the 6th Lord Camoys died. Tom Stonor, a merchant banker, succeeded his father in the Barony of Camoys, determined to do all in his power to save the seat of this ancient Catholic family. He had already valiantly purchased some of the contents at the sale and eventually the family trustees agreed to sell the house and park to him. 'My resources have been stretched to the limit', he said when moving into Stonor. 'Nevertheless, it is tremendously exciting personally and historically that such an old story is to continue.'

It might well seem from this last chapter that the survival of the house has become even more important than the survival of the dynasty in the scheme of things. The two are, of course, inextricably linked; not for nothing are these places called 'family seats'. The historic bricks and mortar have become the symbolic totem poles of the great British families. By the same token, a house without its own family *in situ* is meaningless. Perhaps we should follow the Japanese practice of 'listing' the owner as well as the building; one could well imagine certain territorial magnates being declared 'ancient monuments'.

The great British families have lasted too long for one to write them off at this stage. They have renewed themselves by producing men and women of achievement for generation after generation; it is perfectly possible that they will be able to continue the process so as to provide the country once more with inspiring leadership. The coffin is still empty.

ACKNOWLEDGEMENTS

I WOULD ESPECIALLY like to thank my old friend and collaborator Mark Bence-Jones whose encyclopaedic knowledge and acute insight into the aristocracy has been of the utmost value in writing this book. I am also very grateful to the following for advice and practical assistance: Gillon Aitken, the Knight of Glin, Sarah Greenwood, Norman Hudson, Robert Jarman, Mary Killen, Charles Kidd, Cynthia Lewis, the late Sir Iain Moncreiffe of that Ilk, Bt, the late Patrick Montague-Smith, Caroline Montgomery-Massingberd, John Montgomery-Massingberd, Peter Reid, John Martin Robinson, Hugo Vickers, David Williamson and Carole Winlaw.

HMM

PICTURE CREDITS

Black and white:
BBC Hulton Picture Library: 29, 33, 47, 59, 71(below), 76(above), 111, 133, 139(above), 148(above), 155(above), 171(above), 173, 175, 181(above)
Country Life: 167(below)
Courtauld Institute of Art: 13
ET Archive: 9, 101, 141, 145
The Field: E Crichton 49, S Gupta 187(below), R Mildenhall 67(below), K Sharp 11
Granada Television: 183
HM The Queen: 57, 75, 148(below)
ICI Chemicals and Polymers Group: 111(above)
The Illustrated London News: 89
Dafydd Jones: 33(above), 87(below), 139(below)
The Mansell Collection: 25, 65, 71, 129, 137
Marquess of Hamilton: frontispiece, 171(below)
Marquess of Salisbury: 47
Alistair Morrison: 181(below)
National Galleries of Scotland: 123, 127, 140, 147
National Gallery of Ireland: 159, 161, 165
National Library of Ireland: 155(below), 167(above)
National Monuments Record: 19, 67(above), 87(above), 95(above), 105(below)
National Portrait Gallery: 39, 45
The National Trust: 21, 53
Desmond O'Neill: 109

The Royal Commission on the Ancient & Historical Monuments of Scotland: 143(below)
Royal College of Surgeons of England: 119(above, below)
Scottish Tourist Board: 135, 143(above)
Survival, Anglia: 107
John Tarlton: 187(above)
Times Newspapers Ltd: 179
Victoria & Albert Museum: 35
The Wallace Collection: 51
Weidenfeld & Nicolson Ltd: 55, 76(below), 93(above, below), 95(below), 97, 105(above)

Colour:
The Bridgeman Art Library: 43, 44(above), 79
Daily Telegraph Colour Library: G Germany 44(below), D Kasterine: 41(below)
T Mercer 115, 116(above), S Skelly 78(below)
Duke of Norfolk: 41(above)
The Field: R Mildenhall 80
His Grace The Duke of Beaufort: 42
Alistair Morrison: 150–1
National Galleries of Scotland: 116(below)
National Motor Museum: 113(below)
The National Trust: 77, 78(above), 114
Pieterse-Davison International Ltd: 149
Pilgrim Press: 113(above)
Josiah Wedgwood & Sons Ltd: 152

INDEX